Management for Professionals

The Springer series *Management for Professionals* comprises high-level business and management books for executives. The authors are experienced business professionals and renowned professors who combine scientific background, best practice, and entrepreneurial vision to provide powerful insights into how to achieve business excellence.

Sascha Stürze • Markus Hoyer •
Claudio Righetti • Matthias Rasztar

Agile Marketing Performance Management

10 Success Factors for Maximizing Marketing ROI Dynamically

Foreword by Marc Fischer

Springer

Sascha Stürze
Analyx GmbH
Düsseldorf, Germany

Markus Hoyer
Analyx GmbH
Düsseldorf, Germany

Claudio Righetti
Analyx GmbH
Düsseldorf, Germany

Matthias Rasztar
Dr. August Oetker Nahrungsmittel KG
Bielefeld, Germany

ISSN 2192-8096 ISSN 2192-810X (electronic)
Management for Professionals
ISBN 978-3-658-38052-6 ISBN 978-3-658-38053-3 (eBook)
https://doi.org/10.1007/978-3-658-38053-3

This Springer imprint is published by the registered company Springer Fachmedien Wiesbaden GmbH, part of Springer Nature.
The registered company address is: Abraham-Lincoln-Str. 46, 65189 Wiesbaden, Germany

Foreword

The optimal allocation of resources in marketing, which is necessary, for example, to optimise the media mix, is a perennial issue. Conceptually, the problem is not very complex. However, the concrete implementation raises a number of questions that need to be answered. From projects and discussions with companies across different industries, I have learned that—despite all the differences—there are a number of recurring questions that need to be solved. These include assessing the profitability of activities, i.e. calculating a return on investment (ROI).
Here, it becomes apparent in most projects that it is not so much about the isolated consideration of the ROI of an individual activity or media channel, but rather the holistic assessment, which aims at a better, simultaneous allocation of resources. Paradoxically, the profit contribution of a product portfolio can be significantly increased even if the budget is reduced at the same time if the focus is on optimising the **allocation** of resources.

Measuring the ROI and revenue contribution of marketing activities always assumes that we have knowledge about the effectiveness of the channels and measures. This is not always immediately reflected in sales, but time-delayed effects and the translation of measures via intermediate variables such as brand equity must be taken into account. This measurement is not trivial. Nor is it trivial if you want to take the quality of a campaign into account when measuring effectiveness. Measuring the ROI and revenue contribution of marketing activities always presupposes that we know how effective the channels and activities are.

A lot has happened in these fields in the past. Today, we have better tools and concepts at our disposal.

Finally, with the increasing use of machine learning approaches and artificial intelligence (AI) in general, there is a new class of models that enables completely new applications. We are working very intensively on these approaches in marketing research. Here, too, it is apparent that a deep understanding of the approaches in their diversity is required to select the right algorithm. However, it seems to me that it is almost more important to understand the decision background and the goal of the marketing decisions in advance. Machine learning is solely focused on optimising the forecast. This may be sufficient in certain cases when forecasting accuracy is the explicit goal. But the allocation of resources to departments and brands also requires an understanding of causality that is independent of current conditions. In a political decision-making process, hard budgeting choices need to be well justified. AI methods find their limitations here because they only provide predictions, not explanations.

It is gratifying to see that the authors have dealt so deeply with these various issues from a practical perspective. They take a well-founded position and contribute their extensive experience from a large number of industry projects. Reading this book should provide every marketing decision maker with important insights and knowledge, enabling them to deal with the topic of budgeting even better and more professionally in the future.

Marketing Science and Analytics, University of Cologne
Cologne, Germany

Marc Fischer

University of Technology Sydney, Business School
Sydney, Australia

Acknowledgments

First of all, we would like to thank **Prof. Dr. Marc Fischer**—our scientific advisor—for his constructive review of the content and for pointing out important articles from the current Marketing Science literature. **Dr. Pipa Neumann** was certainly our most critical reviewer. Her combination of marketing background and editing experience was a boon to the clarity of many arguments. Without **Lieve Vos's** patience and tireless work in preparing the graphics, editing, and final proofreading, the book would not have been published in 2022, we thank her very much. Last but definitely not least, we would like to thank the entire **Analyx team**, from whose well-founded work in marketing optimisation for global advertisers we are allowed to quote insights here in anonymised form.

Contents

About the Authors

Sascha Stürze has been working with global CMOs for more than 15 years on making Data Science a standard tool in boardrooms—for the sustainable optimisation of marketing and sales decisions. After his time at McKinsey, he has co-founded a total of seven marketing analytics and AI companies. Sascha is a CPO of Analyx and has—among others—supported ten of the DAX40 companies in this function.

Markus Hoyer has been involved in marketing, brand strategy, and marketing optimisation for almost 20 years. He gained hands-on marketing experience in brand management roles at Procter & Gamble and later applied and expanded his knowledge as a consultant at McKinsey & Company and as Head of Market Research at Forsa in various industries. He knows the power of data for optimised marketing decisions and is equally familiar with the hurdles of practical implementation. Today, he is the COO of Analyx.

Claudio Righetti After his time at McKinsey, he gained over 20 years of experience as a senior manager in the consumer goods industry and, among other things, built the global marketing information system for a multinational manufacturer. From practical experience, he understands both the need for strategic data management and the challenges in implementing international portfolio planning and budget allocation processes. Claudio Righetti is a CEO of Analyx.

Matthias Rasztar is an Executive Manager Marketing Excellence at Dr. August Oetker Nahrungsmittel KG. Matthias headed the European Marketing Mix Modelling Hub incl. advertising research at Unilever for many years and played a key role in driving the ROMI program during this time. Later, as Head of Purchase Controlling, he reported directly to the Board of Management for Merchandise at EDEKA Zentrale AG. Thus, he knows the manufacturer and retail side equally well and is also a proven method expert for panel analytics, shopper research, and big data.

List of Figures

List of Table

Introduction

1

Marketing is facing an increasing pace of change. Consumers adapt their buying, product usage, and communication behaviour more dynamically than in the past. COVID-19 is acting as a catalyst for digitisation and has dramatically accelerated the willingness to buy more and more frequently online—to name just one example.

However, this general change has very different effects depending on the industry, product category, brand, and target group. This makes **optimally allocating marketing budgets between different brands, business units, and the increasingly diverse and fragmented communication channels and activities even more complex**. Times change: advertising on a new social media platform that was very effective the previous year may no longer be so the next.

Under these dynamic conditions, marketers who use modern, data-driven tools to bundle all important information and reliably forecast the effects of future marketing activities are more successful. Today, sophisticated **mathematical-statistical methods in combination with user-friendly tools** can provide important decision-making aids for optimal budget allocation, i.e., for the distribution of the marketing budget among media channels, brands, product groups, and countries. In such a way the best possible sales impact is achieved with tight budgets (maximum return on investment).

Agile marketing means that the allocation decisions made are repeatedly validated on the basis of the newest information in a structured feedback loop and—if necessary—adjusted to new findings instead of just looking things over at the end of a planning cycle. But how do you meet the high demands of agile, dynamic marketing budgeting? How do you tell the difference between meaningful shifts in advertising impact and short-term buzz?

In this book, the authors want to contribute to this by not only critically examining existing approaches but also by presenting relevant state-of-the-art techniques. The book intends to benefit decision makers in marketing and attempts to strike the necessary **balance between theoretically rigorous concepts and the required pragmatism**.

S. Stürze et al., *Agile Marketing Performance Management*, Management for Professionals, https://doi.org/10.1007/978-3-658-38053-3_1

In ten chapters, success factors are presented that are important for anyone who wants to take advantage of agile marketing:

1. **Optimise holistically**: The majority of the potential can only be leveraged by optimising across all activities, brands, and products. If you continue to focus only on the media mix within a brand, you leave more than 50% of the potential untapped.
2. **Explicitly take long-term brand impact into account**: Focusing on short-term sales impact only can lead to significant misallocation. A positive marketing ROI can seldom be established based on short-term impact only. The good news is that the long-term effect of brand equity onto the hard currency of sales can be quantified.
3. **Balance brand building and performance marketing**: Digital advertising is becoming increasingly suitable for brand building under the right conditions, and this can be analysed with appropriate tools. The same is true for finding the optimal balance between image advertising and sales activation.
4. **Campaign-specific measurement**: Spot A is not the same as Spot B, and long-term averages of media channel effectiveness are therefore only of limited help. Copy tests before airing a creative are a good first point of reference. But it is just as important to measure the actual impact of a spot or ad ex-post as part of an overall model. The same model can help identify campaigns with above-average success and thus promote strengthening brand development in a targeted, data-driven way.
5. **Measure forecast quality**: An R^2 (coefficient of determination) of 90% sounds good at first. However, it is more important whether the target variable (e.g. sales) is actually predicted correctly. For this, a broad database, smart procedures, and regular data updates are crucial.
6. **Combine tools in a meaningful way**: Attribution models are not "better" than marketing mix models (MMMs) yet help with the individual fine-tuning of online channels. But only in combination with the helicopter view of an MMM, which calculates an optimal distribution across brands and on the individual channels, can marketing be optimised truly holistically.
7. **Avoid hyper-targeting and build your own consumer data pool**: As sensible as the marketing precision through targeting is in principle: A single-minded focus on an individual targeting of consumers in the lower funnel should be avoided. And in view of the imminent "cookie death", having access to your own, first-party data is urgently required.
8. **Adapt regularly**: The growing dynamics of the market environment and consumer behaviour requires more frequent (e.g. monthly) updates. This is the only way to react quickly when budgets change, the efficiency of a channel declines, or a new spot has a particularly high impact.
9. **Prioritise data collection in meaningful formats**: Databases may not be sexy, but no marketing optimisation can succeed without a clean history of relevant data in sufficient detail and easily processable formats—and while you are at it, organise the process so that regular updates require little effort.

10. **Identify the right partner and service model**: Very few companies have all the in-house data science and research capabilities needed to build the tools and models presented here. Which criteria have proven successful for selecting appropriate service providers, how do I evaluate them, e.g., via scorecards, and what do I want to insource in the medium term, what should remain outsourced?

Each chapter covers the following four aspects:

- Why is the aspect important for successful optimisation?
- What insights does scientific research offer?
- What does corporate practice suggest?
- What recommendations follow from this for marketing managers?

In addition, there are two digressions on some frequently asked questions:

- What happens to sales and brand if I radically cut back on marketing investments? And does this make sense in a recession?
- How useful is zero-based budgeting and how does this approach relate to agile marketing?

Optimised Budget Allocation in Marketing "Beyond Media" 2

Since the days of John Wanamaker, the "father of modern advertising," marketers have been trying to avoid wasting the proverbial half of their budgets.[1] Their endeavours to confront this problem are supported by a number of established, but still mostly fragmented, tools at the level of individual brands in a country. These tools include classic media mix optimisation, customer journey analysis, and various techniques in brand equity management.

Against this backdrop, the result of scientific studies is not surprising: *marketing-induced revenue could be further increased by 15–25%, or overall brand revenue by 1–4%*, by not only optimizing the allocation of marketing budgets within a brand, but by systematically extending the reach of data-driven techniques to budget optimisation between lines, brands, product groups and countries.

Historically, this has been difficult to implement due to technical limitations and data constraints involved. Today, it not only lies within the reach of most companies, but—in the context of the current market and channels dynamics—is a necessity for long-term value enhancement.

The most successful companies in terms of attaining the above potential have anchored such data-driven budget optimisation in *a dynamic, agile planning process*. This allows them to confirm the effect of budget decision and to quickly identify any misallocation. The strategic aspects as well as organisational and methodological success factors to be considered are described in the following sections.

[1] John Wanamaker (1838–1922) was the first to shape the famous quote "Half the money I spend on advertising is wasted; the trouble is I don't know which half." [John Wanamaker Quotes, https://www.quotes.net/quote/18735 (retrieved 13/01/2021)].

S. Stürze et al., *Agile Marketing Performance Management*, Management for Professionals, https://doi.org/10.1007/978-3-658-38053-3_2

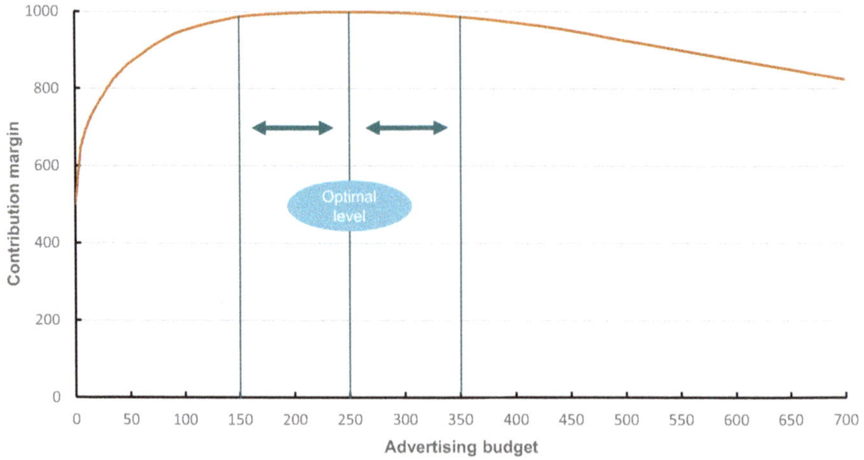

Fig. 2.1 Principle of the flat maximum (Skiera 1997; "Optimal level" indicator added)

2.1 Allocation Is Key!

There is a lot of passionate debate taking place in companies about what the right amount of the *total* budget for marketing and promotional activities ought to be—in other words, its optimal level for achieving certain goals. It may seem counterintuitive at first, but this matters much less (as long as you are in the right target corridor) than the right *allocation* of an existing budget.

This insight is called the "principle of the flat maximum", which goes back to an influential paper by Tull et al. from 1986 (cf. Fig. 2.1).[2] In essence: in the majority of practical situations, *even deviations from the optimal budget level of up to ±25% do not have any significant influence on the contribution margin* of a company.

This is because the higher costs of a marketing budget above the optimal level are almost compensated for by the additional sales and the resulting contribution margins.

In the same way, the loss of sales or contribution margin due to a budget that is *below* the optimal level is almost offset by the lower costs.[3]

It is therefore important to constantly readjust the budget allocation, which then also makes the struggle over the budget level much easier. In short: *Allocation is the more important thing to worry about.*

[2] Tull, D.S./Wood, V.R./Duhan, D./Gillpatrick, T./Robertson, K.R./Helgeson, J.G.: 'Leveraged' Decision Making in Advertising. The Flat Maximum Principle and Its Implications. In: Journal of Marketing Research, Vol. 23, 1986, pp. 25–32.

[3] Skiera, B.: Das Prinzip des flachen Maximums. In: Die Betriebswirtschaft, Vol. 57, 1997, pp. 864–867.

2.2 Allocation Concerns More Than Media Mix

So, let's focus on budget allocation: When it comes to budget allocation *within individual (especially digital) marketing channels*, modern tools are often already in use. In highly targeted channels (e.g., retargeting, search engine marketing), control and thus budget allocation is sometimes left entirely to artificial intelligence, within certain constraints in the form of maximum weekly budgets, etc.[4]

In tactical budget allocation *between different media channels*, statistical methods are used by some companies to isolate the effect of individual channels and use this knowledge to direct the budget to the most effective channels. The abbreviation MMM is often associated with these marketing mix models.[5] MMMs are based on sophisticated econometrics (see Chap. 6), which have recently seen a noticeable renascence, as they do not depend on individual user data or the presence of cookies and also work for channels that cannot be easily targeted to individual consumers, such as TV and billboard advertising.

However, if we look beyond this at how the really "big" decisions are made in corporations with global brand portfolios—namely the distribution of budgets *across brands, product groups, and even countries*—we often find pretty rough-cut approaches:

- Heuristics (e.g., ±5% from last year, 30% for innovations, doubling digital budget each year. . .)
- Finance-based specifications (e.g., percentage distribution according to contribution to sales, profit or growth)
- Strategic priorities (e.g., BCG matrix, focus markets, but also: "Whoever screams loudest . . .")

Ironically, it is precisely the area with the greatest untapped potential, as this chapter will highlight: With a focus purely on media allocation within a brand inside a country (supported by modelling every 2–3 years at best), many companies are clearly falling short (cf. Fig. 2.2).

In order to really take advantage of the sizeable potential for profit increase (see Sect. 2.3), the optimisation of budget allocation must grow in both dimensions of Fig. 2.2:

- *Consideration of as many marketing activities as possible*, i.e., extending horizontally in the above illustration: Ultimately, the aim of using resources in marketing is always to maximise profit in the medium term. This is what brand-building TV campaigns should yield over time, as well as sales activation activities, e.g., new customer goodies in the telecommunications industry.

[4]https://www.criteo.com/technology/ai-engine/predictive-bidding/ (retrieved 18/01/2021).

[5]https://analyx.com/mmm-101-driving-roi-in-a-multi-everything-marketing-reality/ (retrieved 18/01/2021).

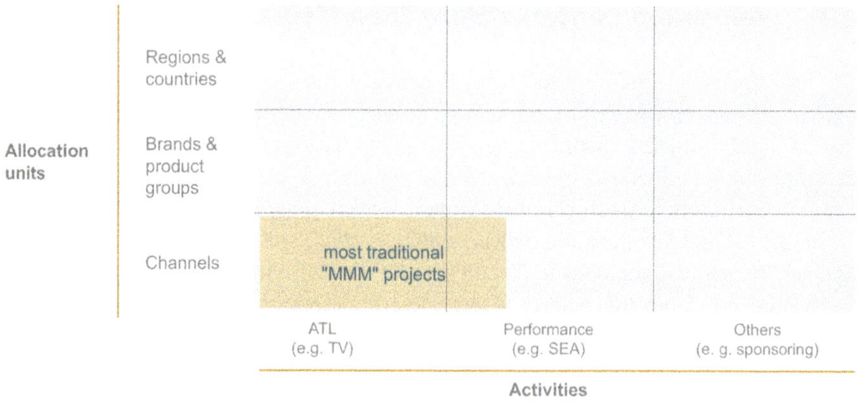

Fig. 2.2 Coverage of traditional marketing mix models (own illustration)

However, budgets are often orchestrated in disconnect and sometimes even inconsistently. A frequently observed example: ATL budgets are allocated on the basis of target KPIs derived from brand tracking, while performance budgets are optimised with an eye on short-term sales increase.

- *Going beyond the channel mix*, i.e., extending vertically in the illustration above: Budget allocation is typically subject to a hierarchy of money distribution from the top (between countries) to the bottom (between channels and campaigns). Media mix—the allocation of money across channels such as TV, Radio, SEA, and Social Media—is focused only on relative advertising effectiveness within a brand. However, the task of budget allocation in a portfolio of multiple brands and countries has to consider more drivers including the different growth dynamics and profitability of the allocation units.

The allocation decisions in an international multi-brand group can quickly become pretty complex, as the following example of a European drug manufacturer shows (cf. Fig. 2.3):

Each year, there are not only 1056 individual decisions being made (whether consciously or not!), but then these decisions also interact with each other. Even for the most experienced managers—equipped with all the necessary data—it will hardly be possible to make these decisions optimally without the use of analytical tools. The wasted EBIT potential, compared to the costs of data-based and tool-supported decision support, is substantial in such situations, as the following practical examples will show.

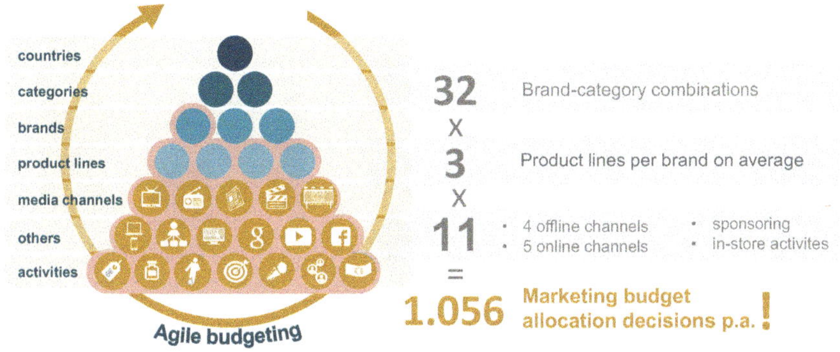

Fig. 2.3 Number of marketing budget decisions in complex organisations (own illustration)

2.3 Global, Cross-Product Budget Allocation Bears Sizeable EBIT Potential

Marketing science has clearly shown that the profit impact is disproportionately higher if the budget allocation is optimised across several of the above-mentioned levels (instead of just between media channels). Probably the most relevant paper on this subject was published in 2011 in partnership with the pharmaceutical company Bayer.[6]

In the year of data collection (2008), Bayer had a budget of around EUR 7.1 billion for marketing and sales (including detailing) in the relevant countries. This included classic media channels (e.g., trade journals) as well as the substantial costs of MD visits by their sales force. The budget was distributed across several core markets and four so-called therapeutic areas (e.g., diabetes). On the basis of econometric optimisation models, a team of marketing scientists developed independent recommendations for the redistribution of budgets at different levels, namely

- between countries
- between therapeutic areas within a country
- between products within a therapeutic area
- between marketing activities for a specific product

The target figure was an economic one, namely the (discounted) profit of the entire business over the next 5 years. The example[7] presented below for the area of

[6]Fischer, M./Albers, S./Wagner, N./Frie, M.: Dynamic marketing budget allocation across countries, products, and marketing activities. In: Marketing Science, Vol. 30(4), 2011, pp. 568–585.

[7]Fischer, M./Albers, S./Wagner, N./Frie, M.: Dynamically Allocating the Marketing Budget. How to Leverage Profits across Markets, Products and Marketing Activities. In: GfK Marketing Intelligence Review, Vol. 4(1), 2012, pp. 50–59.

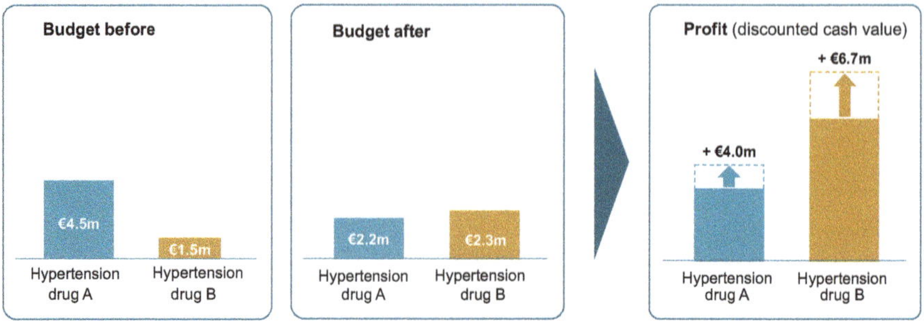

Fig. 2.4 Illustrative representation of the change in budget distribution at Bayer (Fischer et al., 2012)

blood pressure medication shows that the quantitatively derived recommendations in parts deviated quite drastically from the historic budget allocation (cf. Fig. 2.4).

The economic impact speaks for itself and is considerable if applied consistently across all products and countries. In the case of the above-mentioned study at Bayer:

- Potential of EUR 493 million EBIT increase with the implementation of all recommendations (5-year discounted EBIT)
- Impact of EUR 273 million actual EBIT increase within 1 year (2008–2009)

The latter corresponds to an *EBIT increase of 12% in a period in which sales grew by only 4%. The marketing budget itself remained constant.*

2.4 The Bigger Part of EBIT Impact Does NOT Result from Media Allocation

Our own projects with clients from various industries confirm these scientific findings. Just how big the potential can be even within a single country is illustrated by the example of a leading global consumer goods manufacturer, which carried out a project to optimise budget allocation in one of its core markets:

> The goal was to maximise sales by reallocating a constant media budget. About a dozen brands in a total of six product groups and with media investments in five to seven different media channels each were included in the optimisation—in total, more than 100 budget decisions that have to be adjusted several times a year.

First of all, the overall impact: *Engagements like this have the potential to increase sales by just under 2% with a constant media budget*, i.e., through pure reallocation.

In the above example, this corresponds to a sustainable profit increase in the range of double-digit million EUR. But the most important finding here is that *the bigger part of this impact did not come from the traditional area of budget shifts between*

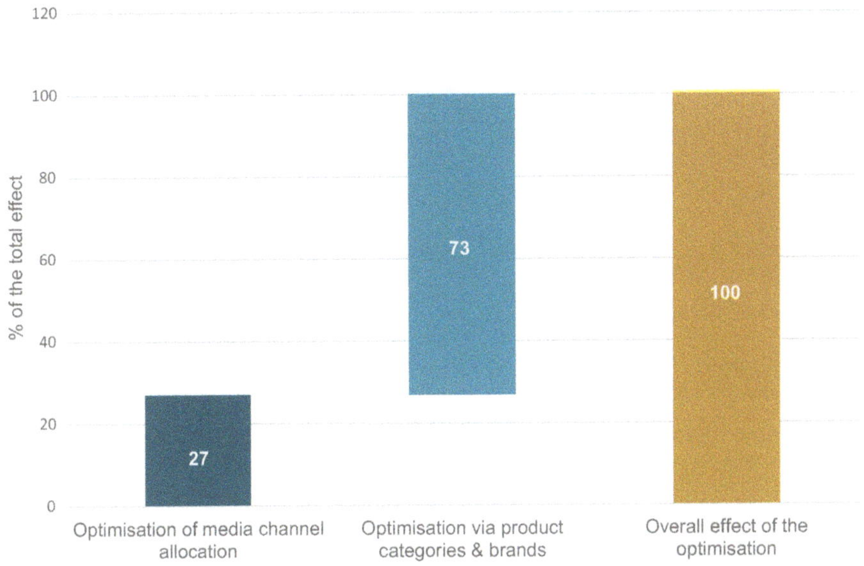

Fig. 2.5 Breakdown of the optimisation impact for a major multi-brand consumer goods manufacturer (own illustration)

media channels, but from budget reallocation between brands and between product lines within brands (see Fig. 2.5).

The allocation recommendations between the brands were—similar to the Bayer example cited above—in part relatively drastic, but intuitive for the client, since they were derived and validated by means of a scientifically confirmed methodology (cf. Fig. 2.6). Here, an optimisation logic was used that traces back directly to the research of Prof. Fischer and his colleagues mentioned above.

As Fig. 2.7 shows, three factors are considered when determining the optimal budget for an allocation unit (e.g., product group X of brand Y in country Z) (cf. Fig. 2.7):

To assure acceptance in corporate environments, it is important that this optimisation logic is not only mathematically validated but also intuitively understandable in terms of the resulting recommendations for action. Here are some examples:

1. *Profit contribution:* All other things being equal, brands or product groups that make a higher absolute contribution to overall profit should receive more marketing budget. An automobile manufacturer supports, for example, the sales of a profitable SUV with more advertising budget than a small car.
2. *Growth:* Likewise—ceteris paribus—brands and/or product groups that are on a steeper organic growth path should receive more marketing budget. This component of the optimisation logic also ensures that innovative new products, which

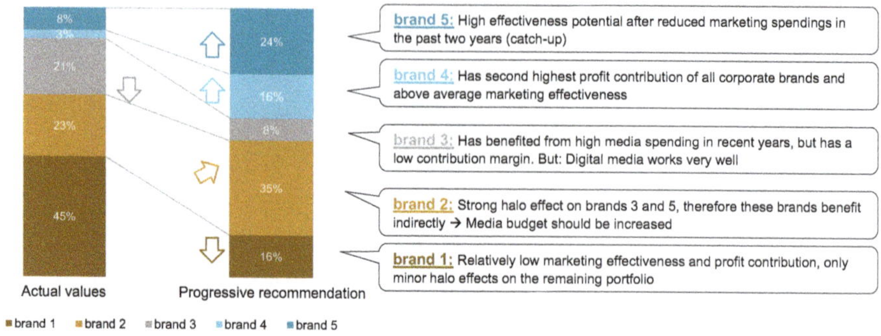

Fig. 2.6 Example of optimised budget allocation for selected brands at a major consumer goods manufacturer (own illustration)

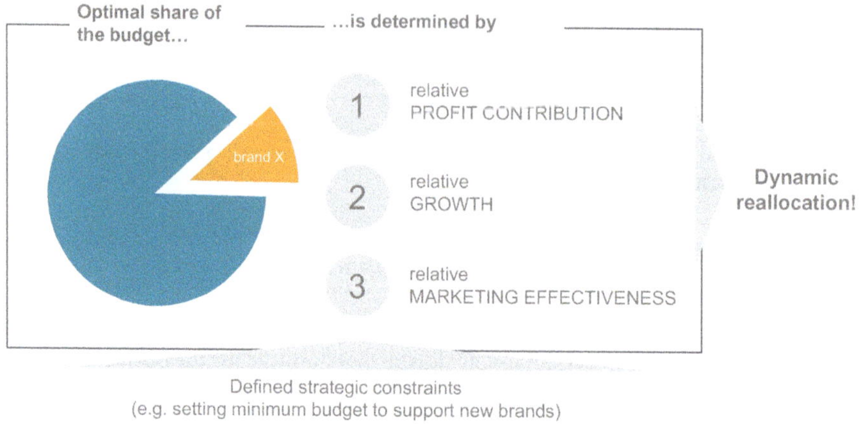

Fig. 2.7 Optimisation logic for portfolio budget allocation (own illustration)

may currently still be making only a small contribution to company profit but are growing rapidly, receive sufficient support.

3. *Marketing effectiveness*: Finally, also ceteris paribus, brands and/or product groups where the use of funds has a higher effectiveness (in terms of mid-term sales impact) should receive more marketing budget.

Leading companies determine the effectiveness of marketing budgets per brand and media channel by means of sophisticated modelling methods (see Chap. 6). These help to isolate the effect of the marketing activities budget from other effects (e.g., seasonality) and thus provide the input for the optimisation presented here.

2.5 Recommendations for Corporate Decision Makers

Optimizing budget allocation in marketing and sales across all relevant levels (countries, product groups, brands, lines, channels. . .) bears enormous potential for increasing marketing ROI. The bigger part of the impact does not stem from an improved media mix (the focus of classic MMMs), but from the levels "above". In a context of historically evolved corporate structures, this is often challenging to implement, as budget allocation is always a contentious issue:

- Responsibility for budget allocation between brands or even countries often lies elsewhere than responsibility for the media mix;
- Even on the level of media mix, one often finds a grown organisational distinction between "ATL/Media/Brand" vs. "Performance/Digital".
- Another barrier is that sales activities/promotions and media activities are only loosely coordinated, thus making holistic optimisation difficult.

However, the above examples show that it is worth leaving these silos behind and to strive for holistic optimisation. In our experience, there are two groups of success factors here, namely organisational and methodological. The methodological factors are by no means purely technical elements for the data science department—they are also critical for the acceptance of data-driven marketing optimisation.

Organisational success factors

Focus on consistent financial KPIs:
Consistent impact assessment based on unit sales/turnover/margin instead of different, inconsistent metrics along the funnel, e.g.,
- Promotional efforts are measured by incremental sales;
- Marketing is measured dominantly by brand KPIs (brand KPIs are and remain highly relevant variables for long-term success, but they must ultimately show a relationship to economic success of the business).

Interdisciplinary cooperation with a coordinating function:
It can make a lot of sense for the CFO reporting line to take this over. The respective (marketing) controllers often have much of the required data available and economic KPIs are their focus.

Integrated planning and optimisation logic across all levels:
Consistent framework (ideally a single integrated one) at HQ level and in local markets; as well as for the budget allocation between brands, product groups and media mix.

Agreement on target variable and explicit goal formulation
Different P&L owners have to agree on the target variable for any modelling (e.g. unit sales) which might be different from the business outcome that should be maximized in optimization. The latter can even change between planning rounds.

Methodological/technical success factors

Strategic guard rails:
Budget allocation optimisation must be able to take into account manually set constraints (e.g., strategic minimum budgets for specific media channels) instead of a "stubborn" mathematical optimisation.

Dynamic reallocation:
The above-mentioned drivers of the optimal budget allocation (relative profit contribution, relative growth, relative marketing effectiveness) are constantly changing. In addition, new budget allocation units (brands, media channels…) are added. Consequently, the budget allocation must also be dynamic and take place regularly, i.e., agile budgeting instead of classic annual planning.

Automation:
In the above example, over 1,056 allocation decisions have to be made annually for 32 brand-market combinations. To do this efficiently, it is recommended to use professional solutions for quick and easy decision support. Another aspect is that Excel or in-house developed solutions often do not even capture the required amount of iterations to arrive at the optimum as they lack computing power. Integrated solution providers can therefore save a lot of time and help to successfully leverage the full potential.

Quantitative Consideration of the Long-Term Effect of Marketing Measures

3

Only the quantification of the long-term effect (measured in sales) enables the calculation of the full return on investment (ROI) of marketing. Nevertheless, many of the currently available approaches are still blind on this eye: many traditional marketing mix models focus on short-term sales effects, while long-term brand equity effects are considered—quite independently—via "soft" target variables such as brand awareness or relevant set.

3.1 Obvious Existence, Difficult Proof

Can you complete these slogans?

- *"Melts In Your Mouth, Not In . . ."*
- *". . .—Gives You WIIINGS"*
- *"Have A Break, Have A . . ."*
- *"Once You Pop, You Can't . . ."*
- *"Just . . ."*

If yes, then you have just confirmed the existence of the long-term effect of marketing (on the dimension of advertising recall). The fact that marketing activities such as TV advertising **also have long-term effects on sales** is a consensus among marketing managers.

However, the exact quantification of this effect is a problem with which science and practical experience have been struggling for about 50 years. In corporate practice, the long-term effect in the context of advertising impact models is often either not quantified at all, or only separately in the form of "soft" KPIs such as brand equity, ad awareness, or recognition. It is far too rarely measured in the "hard" currency of the long-term effects on sales and profits. Given the importance of this, the goal for all marketers should be to have a marketing mix model that incorporates

S. Stürze et al., *Agile Marketing Performance Management*, Management for Professionals, https://doi.org/10.1007/978-3-658-38053-3_3

the long-term effect directly into allocation optimisation. In such cases, one not only has the necessary arguments for the CFO when discussing the required level of the marketing budget and the return on marketing investment. But one can also make much more successful investment decisions about the allocation of funds between brands with different brand strengths.

Why the long-term effect is so important?

1. **Most Offline measures do not achieve a positive ROI in the short term.** Kevin Clancy and Randy Stone, who have been studying marketing ROI for decades, wrote in 2005: "... in the short term, consumer-packaged-goods advertising returns only 54 cents for every dollar invested".[1] Without proof of long-term impact, marketers are in a defensive position and often become the victims of budget cuts in times of crisis or when there is short-term profit pressure.
2. **Budget allocation purely on the basis of short-term effects can result in making the wrong decisions. Optimising only short-term sales may permanently damage brands,** since the long-term effect of some measures (especially ATL) is many times greater than the short-term effect, while other actions have almost only short-term effects (e.g. promotions).

3.2 Marketing Science Provides Long-Term Multipliers

Hundreds of studies on this topic have been conducted: In the 1970s, the focus was on advertising adstock and time-lag coefficients; in the 1980s, brand equity became popular, and in the mid-1990s, "How T.V. Advertising Works"[2] laid a foundation for quantifying the long-term impact that is still relevant today. At that time, an **average long-term multiplier of 1.81 was determined on the basis of 389 experiments**, i.e. the long-term effect is almost as high as the pure short-term effect and can thus almost double the overall effect (calculation: total effect divided by short-term effect = long-term multiplier). In scientific research, the long-term effect is usually referred to as carry-over effect.

Those results were confirmed with almost the same outcome in another study in 2007: over a decade later, the average multiplier was 1.83.[3] Pauwels et al. measured an average of exactly 1.8 across 62 brands studied in 2010, using a different methodology and different data.[4]

[1]Clancy, K. J./Stone, R. L.: Don't Blame the Metrics. https://hbr.org/2005/06/dont-blame-the-metrics (retrieved 21/05/2021).

[2]Lodish, L. M./Abraham, M./Kalmenson, S./Livelsberger, J./Lubetkin, B./Richardson, B./Stevens, M. E.: How T.V. Advertising Works. A Meta-Analysis of 389 Real World Split Cable T.V. Advertising Experiments. In: Journal of Marketing Research, Vol. 32(2), 1995, pp. 125–139.

[3]Hu, Je/Lodish, L. M./Krieger, A.M.: An Analysis of Real World TV Advertising Tests. A 15-Year-Update. In: Journal of Advertising Research, Vol. 47(3), 2007, p. 348.

[4]Srinivasan, S./Vanhuele, M./Pauwels, K.: Mind-Set Metrics in Market Response Models. An Integrative Approach. In: Journal of Marketing Research, Vol. 47(4), 2010, p. 679.

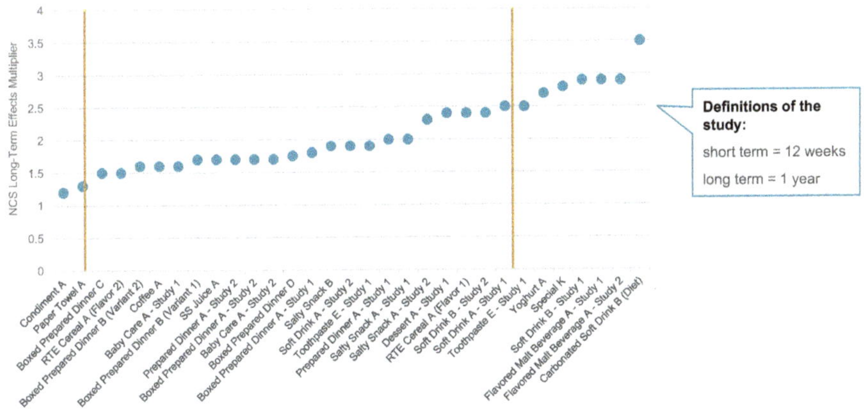

Fig. 3.1 Long-term multipliers for different consumer goods brands (Wood and Poltrack 2015, p. 129)

The most comprehensive current meta-study on the topic was conducted by Köhler et al., it is based on 918 observations, and was published in 2017. In addition to mass media such as TV, direct marketing was also explicitly included. The average multiplier here was as high as 2.54 (i.e. the long-term effect is one and a half times greater than the short-term effect)—while it is 2.1 for mass media.[5]

Is the doubling of the total effect by the long-term factor therefore a kind of law of nature? Unfortunately, it is not possible to simply multiply the short-term effect (e.g. determined in classic MMMs) by two. As always, the devil is in the details (see Fig. 3.1):

- The **definition of short term vs. long term**: In some studies, the effect in the first year was understood as a short-term effect, while the effects in the second and third years were seen as long-term effects. At the other extreme of studies, only week 1 was considered short term, while weeks 2–52 were considered long term.[6] Accordingly, the multipliers cannot be compared across studies, because the shorter the "short term" is defined, the more effect is accounted for by the "long term" and therefore the higher the multiplier. In 2014, Clary and Dyson found values between 1 and 14 in a scientific meta-study.[7] In their meta-study, Köhler

[5]Köhler, C./Mantrala, M. K./Albers, S./Kanuri, V. K.: A Meta-Analysis of Marketing Communication Carryover Effects. In: Journal of Marketing Research, Vol. 54(6), 2017, pp. 990–1008. By the way, in this study the long-term effect is expressed by LTSE ("long-term share of total effect"). This value is 0.607 on average, which corresponds to a multiplier of 2.54 (1/(1−0.607)).

[6]Berk Ataman, M./Van Heerde, H. J./Mela, C. F.: The Long-Term Effect of Marketing Strategy on Brand Sales. In: Journal of Marketing Research, Vol. 47 (October), 2010, p. 877.

[7]Clary, M./Dyson, P.: The Case for Longterm Advertising. In: Admap Magazine, February 2014, http://data2decisions.com/wp-content/uploads/2014/02/ADM_0214_Data2Decisions.pdf/ (retrieved 18/01/2021).

et al. found that on average of 863 measurements, 90% of the total effect was achieved after just under 9 months.[8]

- The **values scatter depending on brand and product category**: Wood and Poltrack found values between 1.2 and 3.5, using a uniform definition of short term vs. long term. However, the multipliers scatter strongly between different categories of consumer goods—see Fig. 3.1 for details.[9]
- **Different marketing measures achieve different multipliers**: For example, Srinivasan et al. find a value of 3.26 for distribution changes vs. 1.9 for promotions.[10] In an analysis by Gain Theory, the values vary by media channel, e.g., 1.0 for pay-per-click (i.e. no long-term effect), 1.24 for social media (24% long-term gain), 1.71 for print, 2.01 for out-of-home, and 2.35 for TV.[11]
- **For new products, the multiplier is on average higher than for established products:** Köhler et al. determined 4.74 for new products and 2.44 for existing ones.[12]

These results were also confirmed in a study conducted together by GfK and SevenOne Media: for 204 analysed brands from 22 product groups, the average long-term ROI (5 years) with a value of 2.65 was 2.3 times the short-term ROI (1 year) of 1.15[13] (cf. Fig. 3.2).

The importance of taking the long-term effect into account in the ROI discussion becomes clear from the following example calculation: If one sets a "true" multiplier of 1.8 only 0.5 points too high or too low (i.e. wrongly assumes 2.3 or 1.3, respectively), one overestimates or underestimates the overall effect by approx. 28%. This is particularly important because the values between brands in a category often show big differences, so that "rules of thumb" are not a valid basis, especially when optimising the budgets of several allocation units.

What else does the strength of the long-term effect depend on? Science has identified a number of factors:

- **Strength of the short-term effect** (using the same definitions for time periods to distinguish between the short-term and the long-term effect): The stronger the

[8] Köhler, C./Mantrala, M. K./Albers, S./Kanuri, V. K.: A Meta-Analysis of Marketing Communication Carryover Effects. In: Journal of Marketing Research, Vol. 54(6), 2017, p. 1005.

[9] Wood, L. L./Poltrack, D. F.: Measuring the Long-Term Effects of Television Advertising. In: Journal of Advertising Research, Vol. 55(2), 2015, p. 129.

[10] Srinivasan, S./Vanhuele, M./Pauwels, K.: Mind-Set Metrics in Market Response Models. An Integrative Approach. In: Journal of Marketing Research, Vol. 47(4), 2010, p. 679.

[11] Chappell, M.: The Long-term Impact of Media Investment, https://www.gaintheory.com/the-long-term-impact-of-media-investment/ (retrieved 13/01/2021).

[12] Köhler, C./Mantrala, M. K./Albers, S./Kanuri, V. K.: A Meta-Analysis of Marketing Communication Carryover Effects. In: Journal of Marketing Research, Vol. 54(6), 2017, p. 1001 ff.

[13] Wildner, R./Modenbach, G.: Über den längerfristigen ROI von TV-Werbung in einer vernetzten Welt. In: GfK Marketing Intelligence Research, Vol. 7(1), 2015, p. 57.

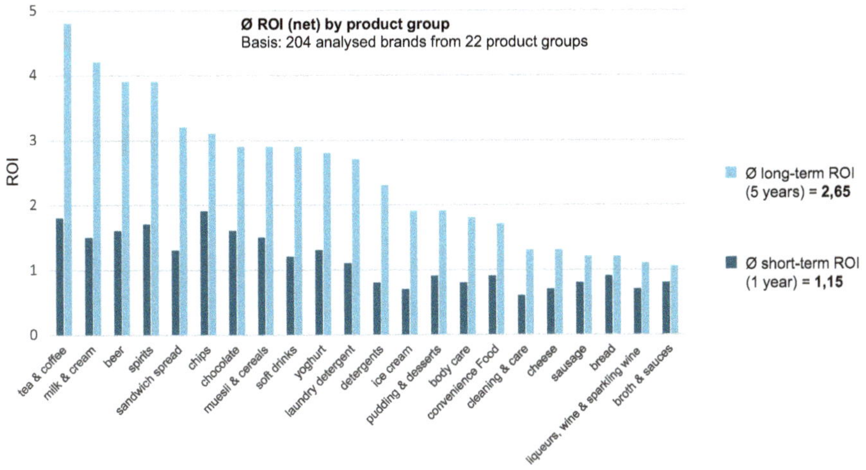

Fig. 3.2 ROI of TV advertising in 22 product groups (Wildner and Modenbach 2015, p. 57)

short-term effect, the stronger the long-term effect (correlation 0.59).[14] Conversely, if there is no short-term effect, there is no long-term effect.[15] The short-term effect is also influenced by a number of factors, including the quality of the copy, advertising expenditure of the campaign, media mix, reach, etc.

- **Level of weekly advertising expenditure in the category:** the higher the total advertising expenditure, the higher the multiplier (correlation 0.52).[16]
- **Purchase frequency (length of the purchase cycle):** The longer the time between two purchases, the lower the long-term multiplier (correlation -0.38).[17]
- **Conversion factor in the brand funnel:** Products with higher conversion rates usually show higher long-term multipliers. Not only a one-time purchase counts, but also changes in brand loyalty (e.g. the change from non-buyer to occasional or repeat buyer). As the buyer moves up the brand loyalty ladder, the likelihood of subsequent purchases of that brand increases and so does the sustainability of the advertising impact.[18]

[14] Wood, L. L./Poltrack, D. F.: Measuring the Long-Term Effects of Television Advertising. In: Journal of Advertising Research, Vol. 55(2), 2015, p. 130.

[15] "[. . .] if TV advertising works in the short term, its impacts are doubled over the next 2 years. If the TV advertising does not work in the first year, it will not have any long-term impact." (Hu, Je/Lodish, L. M./Krieger, A.M.: An Analysis of Real World TV Advertising Tests. A 15-Year-Update. In: Journal of Advertising Research, Vol. 47(3), 2007, p. 348.).

[16] Wood/Poltrack 2015: ibid.

[17] Wood/Poltrack 2015: ibid.

[18] Wildner, R./Modenbach, G.: Über den längerfristigen ROI von TV-Werbung in einer vernetzten Welt. In: GfK Marketing Intelligence Research, Vol. 7(1), 2015, pp. 55–60.

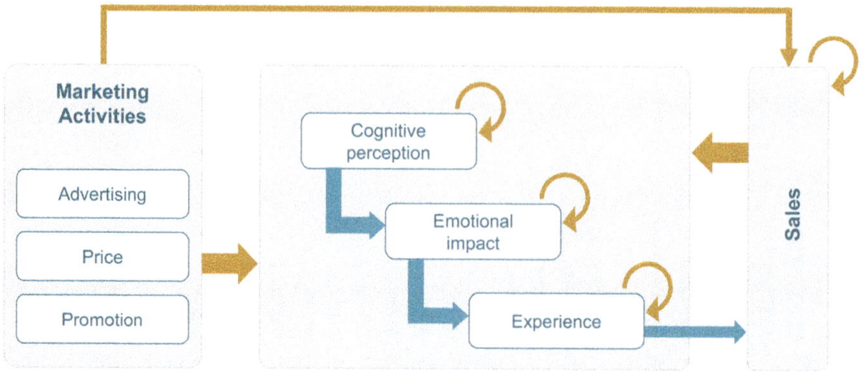

Fig. 3.3 Integration of "mindset metrics" into sales models (translated from Pauwels, K.: How to create KPIs, retrieved on 07/05/2021 from https://analyticdashboards.wordpresscom/2021/02/14/how-to-create-kpis/)

How can the long-term effect be determined? Both in science and in practice, this is **usually operationalised either via carry-over effects or via brand equity (often also called brand goodwill).**[19]

The carry-over approach in the (regression) model directly quantifies the extent to which marketing activities continue to have an after-effect even when they have stopped being on air. The brand equity approach measures separately what buyers know, feel, and experience about a brand. Classic brand KPIs are ad awareness, likeability, and consideration. These can either be directly included in the model as additional influencing variables or indirectly quantified in a two-step process, statistically highly condensed as the influence of brand equity on sales. Step 1 is measuring the effect of marketing activities on brand equity, step 2 is calculating the effect of brand equity on sales.

Brand KPIs can significantly improve marketing mix models: An international research team has shown in a broad study with 62 brands in 4 product categories that the integration of "mindset metrics" (ad awareness, likeability, consideration) in sales models (such as classic MMMs) increases the explained variance by almost one third (cf. Fig. 3.3).[20] Nevertheless, in many cases only carry-over effects are being used, as brand KPIs are often either not available in the necessary temporal granularity (preferably weekly) or they are historically inconsistent.

---

[19]On the measurement of brand equity cf. Hein, S./Schlereth, C./Mueller-Klockmann, T.: Long-Term Brand Equity Measurement. Status Quo and Challenges. In: Transfer, Vol. 65(3), 2019, pp. 6–11.

[20]Srinivasan, S./Vanhuele, M./Pauwels, K.: Mind-Set Metrics in Market Response Models. An Integrative Approach. In: Journal of Marketing Research, Vol. 47(4), 2010, p. 681.

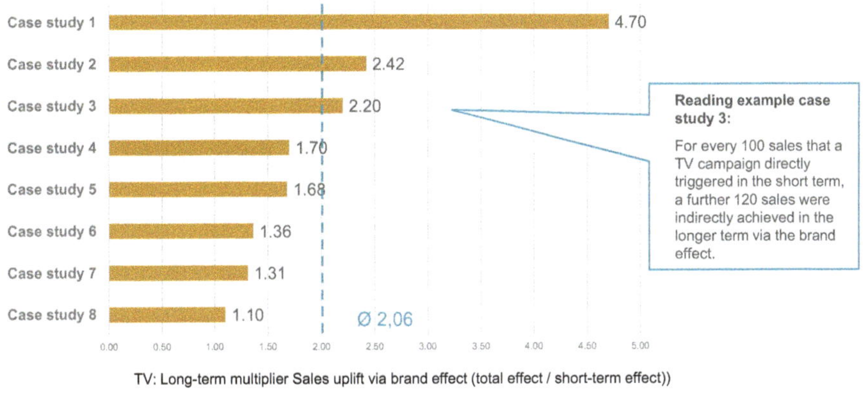

Fig. 3.4 Long-term multiplier of TV advertising, benchmarks from our client projects (own illustration)

3.3 Benchmarks from Practice Show Factor 2 and Broad Spread

Our own projects with clients from different industries confirm the findings of science (cf. Fig. 3.4):

- The average long-term multiplier for TV advertising is in the range of 2, i.e. the **total impact including the longer-term brand impact is about twice as high as the short-term sales uplift.**
- The **range is large even within the same media channel**: For TV, the multipliers vary from just over 1 to over 4, depending on the industry and brand.
- Traditional ATL channels such as TV and out-of-home have on average higher long-term effects than online channels such as SEA or display.

The operationalisation of the long-term impact (2-year perspective) within the framework of our work at Analyx is carried out via what we call the Brand Reservoir (BR). The BR establishes a connection between marketing expenditure and brand KPIs, on the one hand, and sales potential on the other. For this purpose, a structural equation model is created, which is individually adapted for the respective brand or product category. The brand KPIs are usually taken from the high-frequency brand tracker of a data partner (cf. Fig. 3.5).

Only the quantification of the long-term effect in sales enables the calculation of the complete return on marketing investment including the brand effect. The following illustration (cf. Fig. 3.6) shows an example from the consumer goods industry detailing how the total return of two brands (or product variants) is composed. It becomes clear that an exclusive consideration of the short-term return

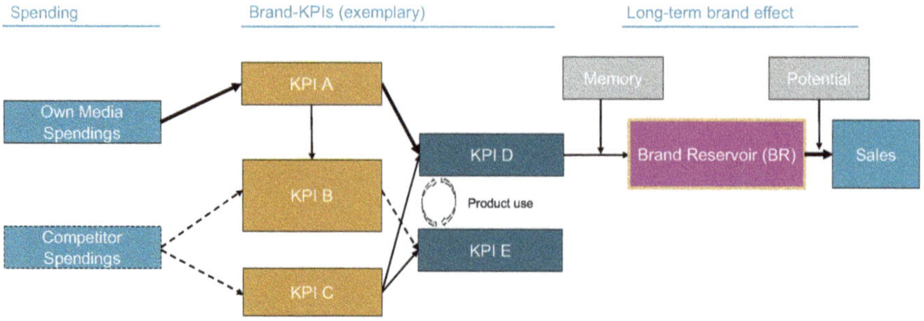

Fig. 3.5 Analyx concept of Brand Reservoir (own illustration)

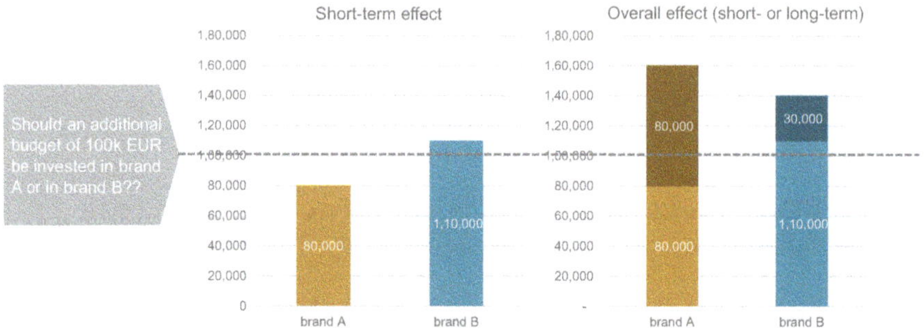

Fig. 3.6 Incremental turnover effects with additional marketing investments (own illustration)

can lead to completely different conclusions and thus misallocations. Accordingly, the ROI of individual media channels can of course also be determined.

3.4 Recommendations for Corporate Decision Makers

Science and our own practical experience confirm that the long-term effect of marketing is a relevant variable in optimisation that should be explicitly gathered. Ignoring it leads to significant misallocations and inefficiencies and can even substantially damage the brand.

However, the assumption of a general "one-size-fits-all" long-term factor is also misleading and should only be considered temporarily in the absence of any measured values. So what concrete steps should be taken?

Organisational success factors

Systematically collect data:
Reliable quantification of the total marketing effect consisting both of short-term and long-term impact requires a data history of at least three years with weekly data. The core building blocks are: detailed sales data, price and promotion data, ATL spends and online KPIs, competitor spend, and relevant brand KPIs.

Explicitly reflect long-term effects when optimising budget allocation:
Only if you know the long-term effect of each measure or channel for a given brand can you really allocate the budget optimally, because some channels only show their full performance when including the long-term view. Therefore, a change from classic, isolated analyses to integrated budget allocation models is the ultimate goal.

Methodological / technical success factors

Use brand KPIs:
While a traditional MMM with a focus on short-term effects could do without brand KPIs, these are very important for modern decision support models including the long-term view in most industries. These brand KPIs are made available via high-frequency advertising tracking (e.g., from YouGov, AdNow, Ipsos, etc.). Of central importance are, among others, ad awareness, consideration, and selected image dimensions (e.g., likeability, value, quality), but also buzz. Ideally, the data should be available in weekly granularity.

Quantify the long-term effect not only on brand, but also on sales:
The long-term effects must ultimately be measured in the same "hard" currency as the short-term effects, i.e., in sales or leads. This requires the combination of traditional MMM elements and brand equity in an integrated overall model.

Striking the Right Balance: Image vs. Performance Marketing

4

A direct implication of the fact that marketing investments have short-term and long-term effects is the question of the right budget allocation between these two essential objectives of marketing:

- Direct sales activation (= performance advertising) vs.
- Branding (=image advertising) for delayed but long-lasting sales activation.

4.1 The Performance Promise

Globally, spending on digital advertising exceeded the level of 50% for **the first time in 2019**. As shown in Fig. 4.1, market experts expect the trend to continue:

In Germany alone, more than EUR 10 billion were spent on digital advertising in total for the first time in 2020, which corresponds to almost half of the total advertising market. More than two-thirds of that was booked programmatically.[1]

Now, of course, rules of thumb such as "digital=performance" and "offline=image" do not necessarily apply anymore (see Sects. 4.3 and 4.5), but nevertheless: the programmatic part of digital advertising in particular often has a kind of built-in performance promise due to its features:

- more specific targeting possibilities down to individual consumers,
- better direct measurement of the effect through intermediate variables such as clicks (see Chap. 8 on these two aspects) and

[1]Duvinage, B.: Digitale Werbung wächst 2020 um 8,6 Prozent, https://www.wuv.de/marketing/digi-tale_werbung_waechst_2020_um_8_6_prozent (retrieved 17/02/2021).

S. Stürze et al., *Agile Marketing Performance Management*, Management for Professionals, https://doi.org/10.1007/978-3-658-38053-3_4

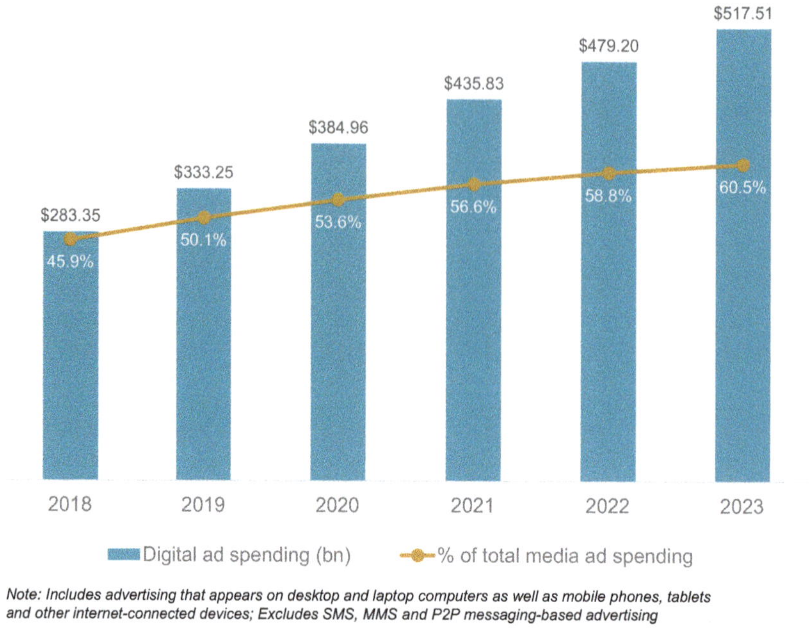

Fig. 4.1 Global digital ad spend and share of ad spend over time (Enberg, J.: Global Digital Ad Spending 2019, retrieved on 17/02/2021, from https://www.emarketer.com/content/global-digital-ad-spending-2019)

- because advertising on most digital channels tends to be closer in time to the consumer's decision to buy ("lower funnel"), a more direct impact on sales can be expected (see Sect. 4.3 on the effect of digital advertising).

This performance promise of digital advertising explains the increasing attractiveness of digital channels also among branded goods manufacturers, who often cannot measure the direct effect of their digital advertising at the individual consumer level in traditional retail. However, the hangover was not a long time coming—Adidas and P&G are probably the most prominent examples:

> The debate about whether the advertising industry has sacrificed the brand on the altar of performance is getting new fuel—and it's coming from Herzogenaurach.[2]

[2]Rentz, I.: Der Fall Adidas verschärft den Kampf der Gattungen, https://www.horizont.net/marketing/nachrichten/performance-vs.-marke-der-fall-adidas-verschaerft-den-kampf-der-gattungen-178503 (retrieved 17/02/2021; translated by authors).

> Adidas admits that a focus on efficiency rather than effectiveness has led to too much focus on ROI and too much investment in performance and digital—at the expense of brand building.[3]

> In 2017, the heyday of digital media has come to an end. This is because of significant waste in an opaque, non-transparent and even fraudulent digital media supply chain.[4]

There can be various reasons why the impact of investments, especially in digital marketing, falls short of expectations in terms of sales impact. These include, for example, the activity of **non-human "bots"**, which generate measurable clicks but are not actually receptive to the advertising messages.[5] Or also non-transparent or **simply exaggerated information on the advertising reach achieved** or other KPIs.[6] The CMO of P&G—Marc Pritchard—addresses these aspects in particular in his criticism of the "media supply chain" quoted above.

A third reason—and Adidas is a good example here—is that the balance between image and performance advertising is maladjusted, and this is to the detriment of mid-term value creation. In more technical terms, **the ratio between investment in short-term sales impact vs. long-term brand impact is suboptimal**. As a result, although some impressive sales successes are achieved in the short term, they fizzle out in the medium period due to insufficient investment in brand image. The following sub-chapters deal with this.

4.2 Where Does Image End, Where Does Performance Begin?

On the one hand, this question can be approached with empirical knowledge. If, for example, marketing decision makers are asked which media channels they think are more suitable for performance marketing and which are more suitable for branding, results are usually similar to the picture shown in Fig. 4.2. This is based on a survey conducted in 2021 by the trade journal Horizont among marketing decision makers in Germany, Austria, and Switzerland:

Over the years, marketing scientists have repeatedly published frameworks that place the various media channels along the well-known marketing funnel. Typically, some media channels (especially TV advertising) are being attributed with a

[3]Vizard, S.: Adidas: We over-invested in digital advertising, https://www.marketingweek.com/adidas-marketing-effectiveness/ (retrieved 17/02/2021).

[4]Pellikan, L: Marc Pritchards Warnung an die Digitalbranche im Wortlaut, https://www.wuv.de/marke-ting/marc_pritchards_warnung_an_die_digitalbranche_im_wortlaut (retrieved 17/02/2021).

[5]Fou, A.: When Big Brands Stopped Spending On Digital Ads, Nothing Happened. Why? https://www.forbes.com/sites/augustinefou/2021/01/02/when-big-brands-stopped-spending-on-digital-ads-nothing-happened-why (retrieved 15/02/2021).

[6]Spangler, T.: Facebook's Sheryl Sandberg Knew About Inflated Ad-Reach Figures for Years, Lawsuit Claims, https://variety.com/2021/digital/news/facebook-sheryl-sandberg-inflated-ad-reach-metric-lawsuit-1234910323/ (retrieved 14/02/2021).

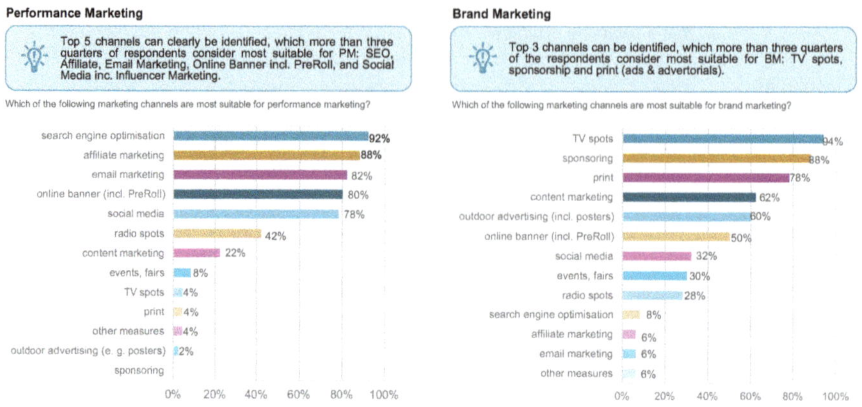

Fig. 4.2 Suitability of media channels for performance and brand marketing [Horizont 2021 (Rentz, I.: Update für eine intensiv geführte Debatte, retrieved on 17/02/2021 from https://www.horizont.net/marketing/nachrichten/brand-vs.-performance-update-fuer-eine-intensiv-gefuehrte-debatte-189174)]

relatively stronger effect in the "upper funnel" (=brand building), while channels such as search engine marketing are more likely to be found to be effective in the "lower funnel" (=sales activation) end of the spectrum. An example of such a framework was presented by Dr. Augustine Fou[7] and is shown in Fig. 4.3.

As you can see, he follows quite a strict view, namely that all digital channels are on the performance side of things. That this is not necessarily the case anymore as we will explore in the following chapter.

4.3 Can Digital Advertising Be Image Building at All?

The short answer is: YES! But not all digital channels have a sizeable brand-building effect, neither do all offline channels (e.g. couponing). Therefore, lists and frameworks like the ones presented in the previous chapter are certainly a first helpful step and for most practical cases they offer good orientation. But they fall short when it comes to a sustainable and regular optimisation of budget allocation. This is not only because new media channels are constantly being added (moving image advertising on TikTok, for example, was unthinkable before 2018/2019), but also, because consumer behaviour in interacting with these channels changes over time.

A good example of this is moving image advertising on digital channels such as YouTube. Following the traditional nomenclature in the previous chapter, one would

[7] Fou, A.: Unified Marketing Framework—When to Use Which Tactic, https://www.forbes.com/sites/augustinefou/2021/01/17/unified-marketing-frameworkwhen-to-use-which-tactic/?sh=1a516574201b (retrieved 12/02/2021).

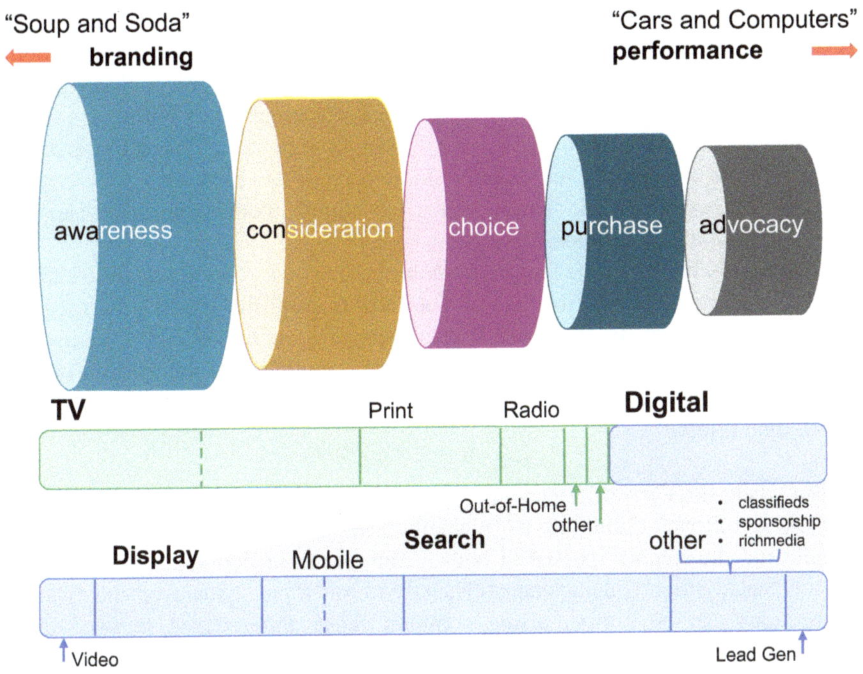

Fig. 4.3 Impact of media channels along the marketing funnel according to (Fou 2021)

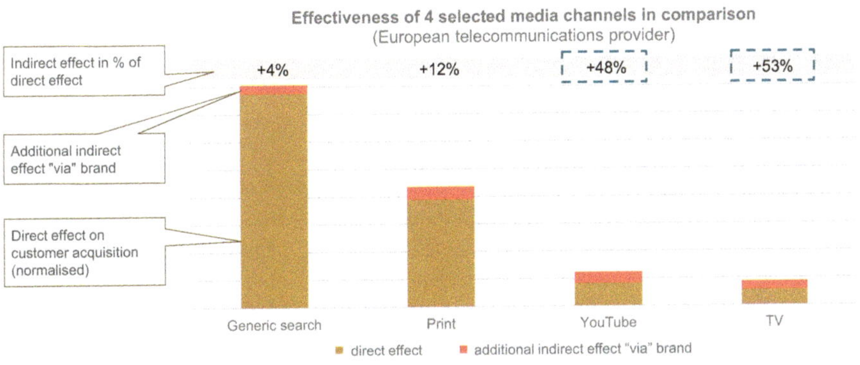

Fig. 4.4 Image-building effect of digital vs. offline media channels (own illustration)

expect YouTube as a digital channel to have a predominantly short-term sales activation effect. However, empirical findings from quantitative modelling increasingly contradict this.

Figure 4.4 is based on a recent marketing mix model by a European telecommunications provider. Four media channels are compared with regard to their effect on sales within the period of 1 year—the higher the column, the more effective the channel—within 12 months:

- It may come as no surprise that search engine advertising (SEA) is by far the most effective channel in this product category. Signing up for a fixed-term mobile phone plan (the standard in Germany is 24 months) is a sizeable monthly budget item. So when the time has come for potential customers to go online in order to search for the product category, they have usually been thinking about this decision for a while and are therefore more receptive to SEA ads.
- YouTube performs significantly worse but slightly better than advertising on traditional linear television.
- In this case, however, the long-term multiplier becomes important (see Chap. 3): This is because **the effectiveness of YouTube is amplified by 48% vs. the pure short-term effect, in the sense that advertising on this channel pushes the brand. This brand multiplier is only slightly smaller than for traditional TV**. Search engine marketing, on the other hand, has almost no measurable brand-building effect.

But where does this difference in brand-building effect between media channels come from? None of the authors of this book is a neuroscientist, so we warmly recommend the recently published book, "The Attention Economy" by Dr. Karen Nelson-Field, which is dedicated exclusively to this topic.[8] However, the essential connections can be grasped using common sense and reduced to two simple statements: **Brand messages are only effective in the medium term if they are "sticky" in the consumers' brain. And they can only be "sticky" if the consumer is willing and able to absorb the messages.**

Attention is therefore the essential concept in Dr. Nelson-Field's work—more precisely, the attention given to advertising messages. A lack of attention in this sense explains why search engine marketing is far less brand building than TV advertising: when consumers search for the category washing machine, it is to be expected that they want information or are comparing prices . The receptiveness for brand messages is thus low at that moment.

Furthermore, clear correlations can be identified between the effectiveness of a media channel and various metrics of attention such as visibility and the undivided concentration of consumers on the respective message. Figure 4.5 illustrates some examples of this. As a measure of effectiveness, Dr. Nelson-Field uses a metric of the sales uplift at a virtual retailer in her experiments called STAS.

Dan White juxtaposed these findings with the average costs of the relevant channels (based on UK data) providing a consistent picture with our own modelling project above and the link to **"Attention" as a core concept** (cf. Fig. 4.6).

The somewhat abbreviated core message is therefore: **Without (as undivided as possible) consumer attention to the advertising message—no brand-building effect**. And the most cost-efficient way of attracting attention is currently still advertising on linear TV, closely followed by Online Video.

[8]Nelson-Field, K.: The Attention Economy and How Media Works: Simple Truths for Marketers, Palgrave Macmillan, 2020.

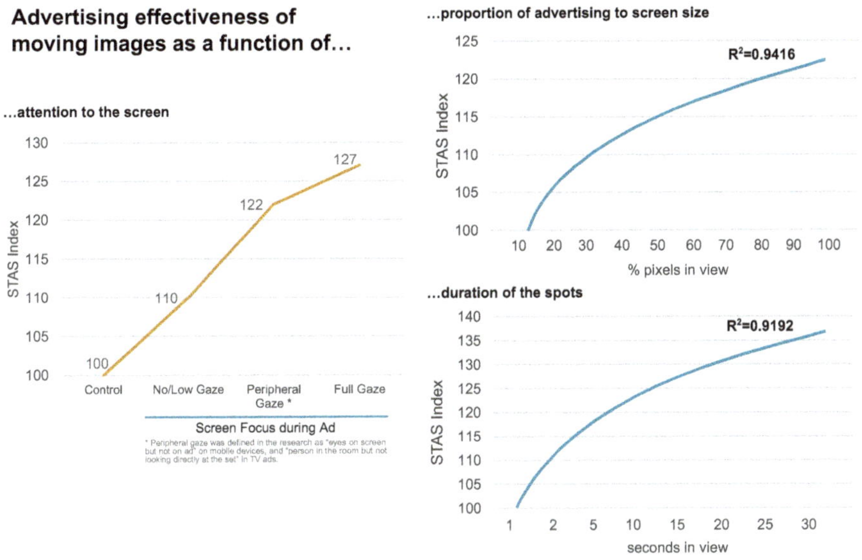

Fig. 4.5 Relationship between advertising effectiveness (y) and various metrics of consumer attention [Dentsu 2019 (Multiple authors: The Attention Economy (White Paper), retrieved on 19/02/2021 from https://www.dentsu.com/attention-economy#top)]

Since this is the case, an exciting question in marketing in the next 5 years will certainly be how marketing decision makers **will be able to substitute the brand-building effect of TV, given that young target groups, in particular, are watching less and less linear TV**.

4.4 But How to Find the Optimal Balance?

Let us return to the optimal budget allocation between image and performance. Using data from young e-commerce companies, Marketing scientists have worked out (cf. Fig. 4.7) that sales growth can be achieved by solely relying on performance channels—at least up to a certain point beyond which sales tend to flatten without investing in brand-building activities:

From that moment on, the question of the right balance in budget allocation is highly relevant in order to avoid the Adidas trap mentioned above. Marketing decision makers often work with rules of thumb such as:

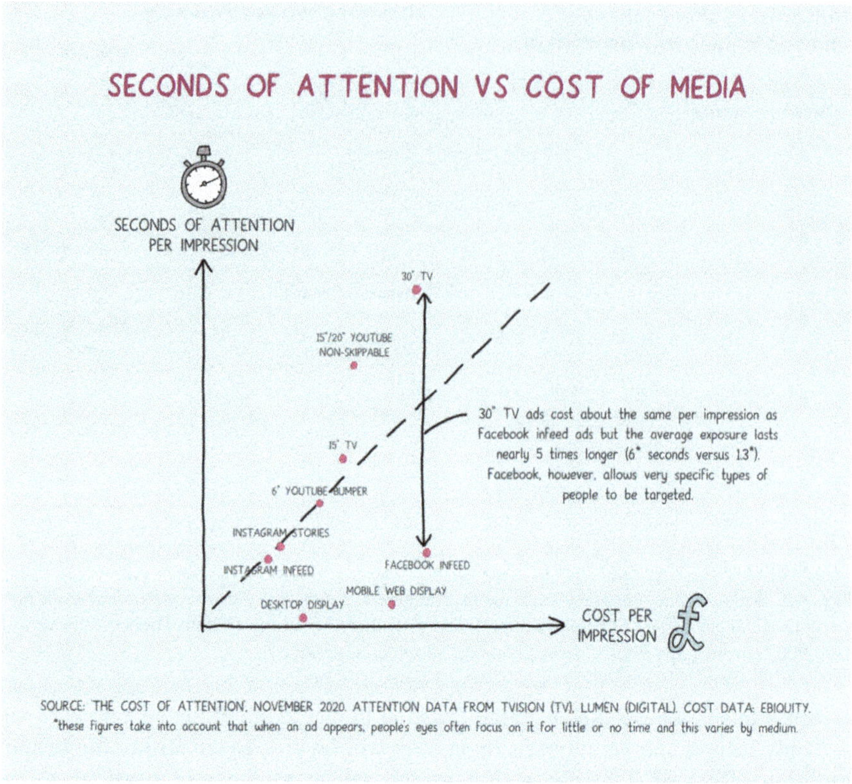

Fig. 4.6 Attention vs. media costs [White, D.: The Smart Marketing Book: The Definitive Guide to Effective Marketing Strategies, LID Publishing, 2020; excerpt of the book provided at https://www.linkedin.com/posts/danwhite1000_smartmarketingdw-marketing-branding-activity-6747552267248918528-twry (retrieved 10/02/2021)]

- 50% performance/50% image,[9]
- always set aside 10% of the budget to support innovative brands,[10]
- or similar heuristics.

However, modern modelling opens up the possibility of driving the outcome of a decision much closer to the optimum—and also to regularly review it based on data. The prerequisite here is above all the clean incorporation of the medium-term effect of advertising on brand strength as well as a quantification of the sales effect of the brand as described in Chap. 3. If modelling supports this, it can also objectively and

[9]Rentz, I.: "Performance-Marketing ohne Investments in die Marke ist nicht zielführend", https://www.horizont.net/marketing/nachrichten/debatte-zur-mediastrategie-performance-marketing-ohne-investments-in-die-marke-ist-nicht-zielfuehrend-178646 (retrieved 17/02/2021).

[10]Robertson, G.: Zero-based budgeting works in theory, but not in reality, https://beloved-brands.com/2019/03/16/zero-based-budgeting/ (retrieved 18/02/2021).

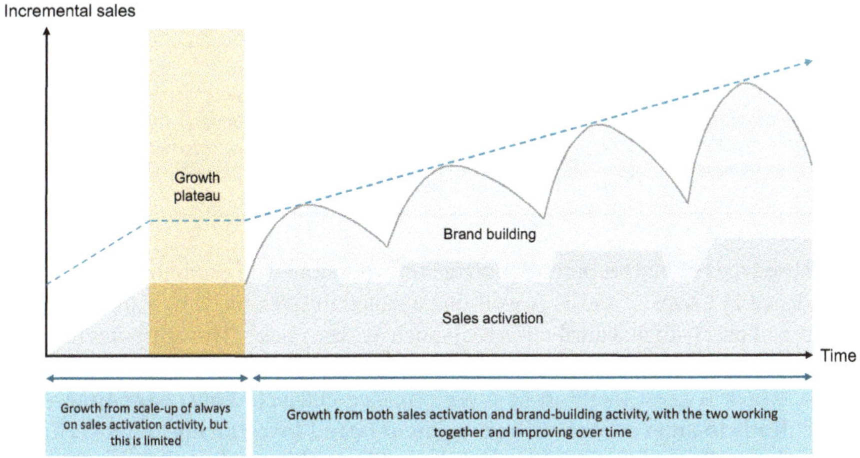

Fig. 4.7 Growth plateau from which brand building becomes vital for further growth [Kite & Roach 2020 (Roach T.: Scaling up without screwing up, retrieved on 03/02/2021 from https://thetomro-ach.com/2020/12/30/scaling-up-without-screwing-up/)]

accurately answer the question of the optimal balance. As a side effect, it becomes *unnecessary* for marketing to decide a priori which channels are image building and which ones "only" promote sales (as explained in Sect. 4.2).

Instead, it is a ***result* of the modelling which determines the types of effects each channel has**. On this basis, a (regular) optimisation of the budget allocation between image and performance becomes just as possible as an optimisation of the allocation to different brands and product groups (see Chap. 2). This can be operationalised, for example, in such a way that **budget optimisation has a long-term objective (= the optimisation criterion) and this is flanked by a short-term guard rail**—as in the following example:

Objective	Secondary condition (guard rail)	Result
Maximise the achievable sales volume over the next three years (=sum of short-term performance effect and long-term effect "via" brand)	*However, sales in the coming 6 months must at least on previous year's level.*	Budget allocation with as much performance share so that short-term sales do not collapse, but long-term goals are achieved

Alternatively, marketing may decide to pursue short-term goals without losing sight of the long-term impact:

Objective	Secondary condition (guard rail)	Result
Maximise the achievable sales volume over the next six months	*However, brand equity should not fall below its current value if we use the optimised marketing mix for the next 3 years.*	Budget allocation with a high-performance share, but sufficient image advertising to support the brand in the long run

These types of budget optimisation are only possible with econometric models as introduced in Chaps. 2 and 3. A well-documented mistake made by Adidas was the overuse of purely digital attribution tools such as "last click". This attributes the sales impact of an observed purchase exclusively to the last touchpoint before the purchase, which is most likely to be a performance channel. **Thus, over time, "last click" leads to an ever-increasing erosion of brand investments and a verifiable suboptimal allocation of budgets**[11] (for further details on this, see Chap. 8).

4.5 "Seeding" Makes No Sense Without "Harvesting"

In all considerations about the optimal budget allocation between brand building and short-term sales activation, it should not be forgotten that these are not binary decisions. In other words: **the momentum generated by image-building investments must be harvested in the lower funnel**. The performance effect that is desired, for example, by investing into search engine marketing, only occurs if the touchpoints even lower in the funnel (e.g. the user experience in the shop) also match the promise. In short: a strategy of "full-funnel marketing" is necessary.[12]

One of the best-case studies of this goes back to the time when compact digital cameras were not yet substituted by smartphones to the same extent as these are today: In the mid-2000s, Kodak made sizeable investments to build brand awareness in this category. Almost the entire digital advertising budget was spent on display advertising to increase brand awareness, but also to raise awareness of the digital camera category as a whole.

What Kodak did not notice was that consumers were not so much looking for the brand name in this category as for the category itself ("digital camera") in order to obtain broader information in light of high device costs. Figure 4.8 shows the relative frequencies per search term at the time:

---

[11] Haan, E./Wiesel, T./Pauwels, K.: The effectiveness of different forms of online advertising for purchase conversion in a multiple-channel attribution framework, In: International Journal of Research in Marketing, Vol. 33(3), 2016, pp. 491–507.

[12] Ader, J./Boudet, J./Brodherson, M./Robinson, K.: Why every business needs a full-funnel marketing strategy, https://www.mckinsey.com/business-functions/marketing-and-sales/our-insights/why-every-business-needs-a-full-funnel-marketing-strategy (retrieved 17/04/2021).

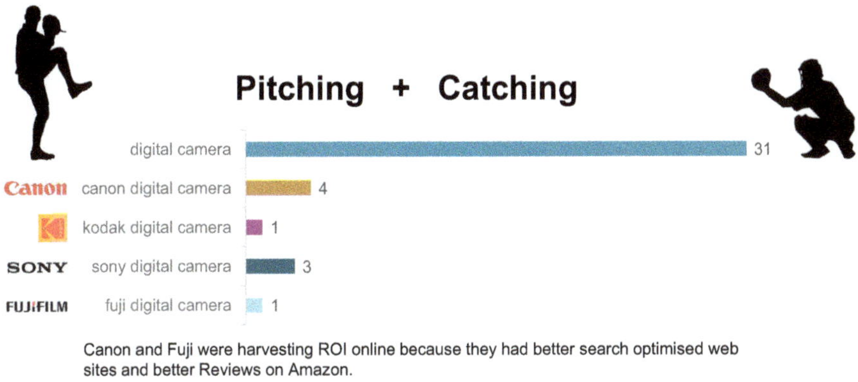

Fig. 4.8 Digital camera manufacturer case study and relative search frequencies (Fou, A.: Digital Marketing Is Like Baseball – Mostly the Catching Part, retrieved on 13/02/2021 from https://www.forbes.com/sites/augustinefou/2020/09/18/digital-marketing-is-like-baseball-most-ly-the-catching-part/?sh=2cca2beb6317)

However, since Kodak's competitors Canon and Fuji had better optimised websites then and also more reviews on Amazon, their search rank put them distinctly ahead of Kodak in a generic Google search. In the end, they were able to reap the benefits in the lower funnel that Kodak had laid the groundwork for with high investments in the upper funnel.

4.6 Recommendations for Corporate Decision Makers

With the support of quantitative methods, the question of "brand vs. performance" no longer has to be a gut decision. However, some success factors need to be taken into account here, which are most certainly not only of technical/methodological nature.

Organisational success factors

Brand & performance at the same table:
Brand building and performance marketing are not opposites. They serve the same goal: a medium-term maximisation of the company's profit. With the right instruments (modelling incl. brand effect), the right budget allocation can be found objectively. But fine tuning within performance (e.g., the selection of the most effective search terms, etc.) should remain a decentralised responsibility.

Coordinate "pitching" & "catching" regularly:
Even with an optimised budget allocation based on perfectly trained models, frictional losses can occur as described at Kodak. Poorly optimised websites or missing reviews on Amazon are less a question of marketing budget than of internal coordination.

Without brand building, it won't work in the medium term:
Digital-first companies in particular often take the view that sales activation via performance marketing can be sustained for a very long time without any investment in brand building. This is verifiably wrong - strategic considerations should not be put on the back burner.

Methodological / technical success factors

Avoid rules of thumb and heuristics:
If possible, CMOs should not rely too much on experiential rules like "digital = performance". Certainly, retargeting will always be a performance channel, as it focuses on already interested buyers and wants to drive them to conversion. But as the example above on YouTube shows: it is better to let solid models instead of gut feel tell you what pays off for the brand and what does not.

Pay attention to spill-over effects:
When evaluating model results, it is important to bear in mind that image-building advertising campaigns can also have spill-over effects on performance channels. The best example: consumers see a commercial on TV, reach for the iPad and search for the advertised brand on Google. Was that driven by TV or SEA? It is imperative to exclude such a spill-over effect from the pure SEA effect in order to avoid budget misallocations.

Digression I: What Happens When Brands "Go Dark", for Example, in a Recession?

Answers to this question tend to depend very much on the industry (e.g. consumer goods vs. capital goods) and the maturity of the brand in question (see Chap. 3). Nevertheless, the renowned marketing scientist Prof. Koen Pauwels has summarised the central academic findings in a blog post.[13] His remarks refer primarily to B2C industries:

- In the short term, the following sales declines can be expected:
  - 5–10% decline for well-established, well-known brands,
  - in the range of 10–30% for young, less well-known brands,
  - for just recently launched products the decline can average 45%.
- The medium- to long-term decline in sales is typically twice as high as the short-term effect.
- In addition to the declining attention of consumers, it is also important to consider the missing signal effect of advertising for investors, trade partners, suppliers, and (future) employees—advertising also keeps the conversation about a brand going.
- The absence of advertising in the upper funnel (brand-building image advertising—see Chap. 4) makes sales activation in the lower funnel—i.e. convincing undecided consumers—more difficult. The conversion rate drops.
- When advertising intensity is ramped up again after some time, there is typically a period of 1–4 weeks before the sales effect of advertising resumes (depending on the respective consumer journey of the industry).

A very recent longitudinal study from the renowned Ehrenberg-Bass Institute for Marketing Science[14] arrives at similar conclusions, although the sales declines upon "going dark" were measured as more severe:

- When brands stop advertising for a year or more, we find sales often decline year-on-year following the stop (on average, sales fell by 16% after 1 year, and by 25% after 2 years).
- The rate of decrease is fastest for brands that were already declining before the advertising stop.
- Brand size also matters. Small brands typically suffer greater declines than bigger brands.

(continued)

[13] Pauwels, K.: What happens if you turn off all advertising for a while? https://www.linkedin.com/feed/update/urn:li:activity:6737445597529341952/ (retrieved 14/03/2021).

[14] Gelzinis, A./Kennedy, R./Beal, V./Hartnett, N./Sharp, B.: What happens to sales when brands stop advertising for long periods? https://www.marketingscience.info/when-brands-stop-advertising/ (retrieved 06/03/2022).

- Bigger growing brands tend to continue to grow after advertising stops for 1–2 years, whereas the sales trend quickly reverses for small growing brands.

Upshot: Especially for long-established brands, completely switching off advertising for a certain period of time can be a profit-maximising strategy. Companies with a broad brand portfolio actually make use of this finding to alternate advertising on different—sometimes competing—brands in regular intervals. Switching off is problematic for young brands and unestablished innovations. Ultimately, CMOs must also bear in mind that the process of winning back market share is an expensive uphill battle.

Should Advertising Budgets Be Cut in a Recession?

There is no rule of thumb for this either. But the criteria for budget allocation to brands or product groups presented in Chap. 2 are very helpful in making such a decision:

1. profitability,
2. organic growth, and
3. marketing effectiveness.

In a recession, the first two indicators can be expected to decline for most consumer products. This means that if marketing effectiveness—i.e. the effectiveness of advertising on sales—remains the same in a crisis, but the other two criteria decline, marketing expenditure should be reduced.

However, there are valid reasons why advertising effectiveness can be *higher* in a crisis than before:

- The same budget buys a higher share of voice as competition is reduced.
- The same budget buys more advertising power, as prices fall.
- The advertised brand is particularly attractive (e.g. because it is inexpensive).

Based on this logic, it would have been optimal for some consumer goods companies not to cut their budgets during the Corona pandemic, as large gains in market share could have been possible for fairly little money.[15]

[15] Kumar, N./Pauwels, K.: Don't Cut your Marketing Budget in a Recession, https://hbr.org/2020/08/dont-cut-your-marketing-budget-in-a-recession (retrieved 16/03/2021).

5 Campaign Tracking and Successful Marketing Controlling

The positive impact of the optimisation recommendations for the marketing budget can be markedly increased if—instead of referring to the average historical impact of a marketing activity (e.g. TV advertising)—the sales impact of individual campaigns is taken into account.

5.1 Campaign-Specific Analyses Instead of Average Effectiveness

There is plenty of proof that advertising has an effect on sales.[1] But it has also been shown that sales does react more strongly to some campaigns than to others. Scientific studies show[2] that the media effect varies greatly.[3] To illustrate this, Fig. 5.1 uses the example of a financial services company to show how differently individual TV campaigns can work.

The analysis of the TV campaigns shows that the campaign impact (here determined by the cost per sale per campaign) varies greatly. An average of all eight campaigns based on historical data would lead to a distorted picture if the underlying campaigns differed strongly in terms of strategy and advertising expenditure.

The reasons for these differences in campaign effectiveness can be manifold:

[1] Sharp, B.: How brands grow, Oxford University Press, 2010.

[2] Tellis, G. J.: Generalizations about Advertising Effectiveness in Markets, In: Journal of Advertising Research, Vol. 49(2), 2009, pp. 240–245.

[3] Assmus, G./Farley, J. U./Lehmann, D. R.: How Advertising Affects Sales. Meta-analysis of Econo-metric Results. In: Journal of Marketing Research, Vol. 21(1), 1984, pp. 65–74.

S. Stürze et al., *Agile Marketing Performance Management*, Management for Professionals, https://doi.org/10.1007/978-3-658-38053-3_5

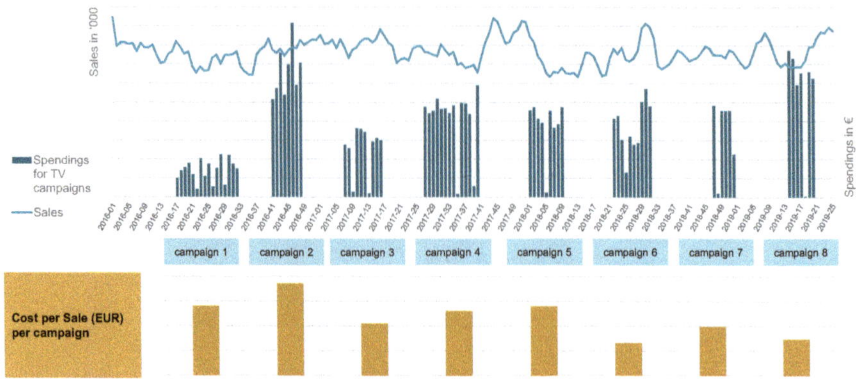

Fig. 5.1 Cost per sale (definition of cost per sale: total expenditure per campaign divided by the number of additional contracts concluded and attributable to the campaign) of various advertising campaigns (own illustration)

- Execution[4]
- Persuasion[5]
- Media mix[6]
- Marketing budget size
- Copy quality[7]
- Competitor activities
- Media plan[8]
- Targeting
- Product Life Cycle[9]

[4]When it Comes to Advertising Effectiveness, What is Key? https://www.nielsen.com/us/en/insights/article/2017/when-it-comes-to-advertising-effectiveness-what-is-key/ (retrieved 13/01/2021).

[5]Sharp, B.: How brands grow, Oxford University Press, 2010, pp. 134–152.

[6]BrandScience/IP Deutschland: Aspekte der Werbewirkung von TV. Eine ROI-Meta-Analyse aus mehr als 300 Modeling-Projekten, 2012, https://docplayer.org/37817328-Brandscience-aspekte-der-werbe-wirkung-von-tv-eine-roi-meta-analyse-aus-mehr-als-300-modelling-projekten-frankfurt-m.html (retrieved 13/01/2021).

[7]Chilian, B./Fleuchhaus, R./von Keitz, B.: Werbetests. Haben sie etwas mit dem Markterfolg zu tun? In: Planung & Analyse, Vol. 17(3), 2000, S. 16–21; Some more selected articles on the current discussion: https://adage.com/article/cmo-strategy/speed-digital-putting-copy-testing-test/300338/ (retrieved 13/01/2021); https://www.wordstream.com/blog/ws/2019/11/25/copy-testing (retrieved 13/01/2021).

[8]"Continuous advertising is more effective than bursts followed by long gaps, because it counteracts memory decay." [Sharp, B.: How brands grow, Oxford University Press, 2010, p. 144.]

[9]Assmus, G./Farley, J. U./Lehmann, D. R.: How Advertising Affects Sales. Meta-analysis of Econo-metric Results. In: Journal of Marketing Research, Vol. 21(1), 1984, pp. 65–74.

- Daytime/Primetime[10]
- Attention intensity[11]
- Marketing strategy (e.g. image or sales campaign)

Advertising campaigns have different effects depending on the marketing strategy (but also depending on the product category, brand, budget level, media mix, or copy quality). For example, the sales impact of an image campaign should not necessarily be compared with a launch campaign. In reality (and in most classic MMMs), such differences are often completely ignored, i.e. either average or maximum values per media channel are assumed. **However, given the variance in effectiveness, advertising campaigns should always be examined individually and in light of their strategic intent (e.g. image vs. sales)**.

In consequence: To make campaigns comparable, not only marketing strategy and advertising pressure should be considered. Care should also be taken to choose the right levels of comparison, i.e. it is advisable to compare TV with TV and within TV to compare launch campaigns with launch campaigns, image campaigns with image campaigns, etc.

It is not a simple endeavour to correctly assess the effectiveness of single campaigns. But methodologically and technically, it is quite possible as we will illustrate in this chapter. In this way, a campaign-specific analysis can be used to find out **which campaign was particularly efficient and should therefore be given greater weight in the future marketing plan**. Another important advantage of the campaign-specific analysis is that the sales effects of alternative campaigns can be simulated on a data basis for the planning of new campaigns. Especially in combination with copy tests, the expected effects can be estimated very precisely, as Sect. 5.3 will show.

5.2 Marketing Controlling in the Context of Dynamic Channel Development

Another challenge for marketers is the constant **change in the media consumption behaviour of consumer groups** and the associated inflation of available media channels, especially in the digital realm. Marketing controllers want to ensure that,

- these new channels are included in the mix optimisation at an early stage on the basis of initial advertising elasticities,

[10] BrandScience/IP Deutschland: Aspekte der Werbewirkung von TV. Eine ROI-Meta-Analyse aus mehr als 300 Modeling-Projekten, 2012, https://docplayer.org/37817328-Brandscience-aspekte-der-werbe-wirkung-von-tv-eine-roi-meta-analyse-aus-mehr-als-300-modelling-projekten-frankfurt-m.html (retrieved 13/01/2021).

[11] Von Keitz, B.: Wirksame Fernsehwerbung, 1. Auflage, Physica; 1983.

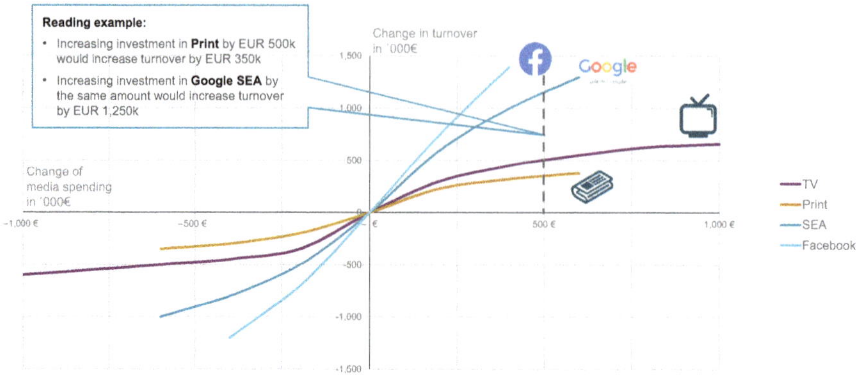

Fig. 5.2 Sensitivity of selected media channels (own illustration)

- their advertising effects are analysed and assessed dynamically and regularly as their share of expenditure increases, in order to prevent "overspend" (i.e. inefficient incremental expenditure),
- in case of (temporary) suboptimal results, especially "immature" channels only get a second chance if their (previous) weaknesses and limitations are known (e.g. suboptimal copy for the new channel, improved targeting expected by new media partner, etc.).

A dynamic view of the underlying sensitivity curves (typically based on solid modelling, see Chap. 6) is critical for success. The following example shows the development of these effects for selected media channels at different media investment levels within 12 months (cf. Fig. 5.2):

In principle, a high number of media channels or advertising formats within a channel (such as YouTube Bumper vs. True-view) does not pose a methodological problem for an econometric model. Each statistically confirmed channel is included in the model with its specific weight. Other channels such as TikTok, Instagram, etc., can be added to a model only after a few campaigns have been observed with a sufficiently high number of data points, variance in intensity, and spending levels.

5.3 The Role of Pre-tests and Campaign Tracking

Many companies only go "on air" with a commercial if it reaches the required threshold values in a standardised pre-test. Operationalisation usually takes place via selected parameters such as uniqueness, likeability, value perception, purchase intention, or recall.

However, practice shows that not every advertising campaign with adequate pre-test values actually generates incremental sales. Also, spots with similar pre-test results often achieve very different sales effects. The reasons are manifold and can be embedded in the test methodology as well as in the overall context of the actual campaign (e.g. media investment level, interaction with other advertising media, or competitor activities).

The consideration of copy quality in campaign tracking helps both strategic marketing, which is responsible for brand management and advertising development, and marketing controlling in the evaluation of marketing investments (ROI).

Scientific studies,[12] as well as market research institutes specialising in advertising research,[13] have been pointing for decades at the necessity of measuring the advertising impact[14] and that there is a **connection between copy quality and sales**. Therefore, from a methodological point of view, it makes sense to take selected advertising dimensions of copy quality into account in an advertising effectiveness model, either individually or in condensed form, e.g., as awareness or effectiveness index, e.g., whenever this data has been systematically collected and is available over a longer period of time.

Standardised advertising tests or trackings measure the expected or real impact of advertising on the basis of strategic advertising dimensions (e.g. recall,[15] persuasion,[16] or likeability[17]). The advertising dimensions are subject to systematic comparisons (benchmarking) in the competitive environment. Benchmarking thus allows to draw conclusions about the defined strategic goals of an advertising campaign (e.g. increasing sales or expanding the image of a brand). What all these advertising tests and trackings cannot achieve is a quantification of the *incremental* sales effect of an advertising campaign adjusted for other external effects, i.e., they can only measure the impact of advertising on the selected dimensions/KPIs of advertising quality, but not make a statement on the sales impact in terms of quantity or value. This can only be achieved by an econometric method that creates the basis for a systematic analysis and ROI evaluation (see Chap. 6).

---

[12] Chilian, B./Fleuchhaus, R./von Keitz, B.: Werbetests. Haben sie etwas mit dem Markterfolg zu tun? In: Planung&Analyse, Vol. 17(3), 2000, pp. 16–21.; and "The major finding was that the quality of advertising was much more important than the quantity: variation in the quality of advertising copy was an order of magnitude more important than the effect of advertising expenditure." [Leach, D. F./Reekie, W. D.: A natural experiment of the effect of advertising on sales. The SASOL case, In: Applied Economics, Vol. 28(9), 1996, pp. 1081–1091.]

[13] Von Keitz, B.: Der Erfolg der apparativen Marktforschung. Basis und Status. In: Transfer Werbeforschung & Praxis: Zeitschrift für Werbung, Kommunikation und Markenführung, Vol. 58(2), 2012, S. 32–40; sowie: Fuchs, W./Unger, F.: Management der Marketing Kommunikation, 5. Auflage, Springer, 2014.

[14] Esch, F.-R.: Werbewirkungsforschung. In: Herrmann, A./Homburg, C. (Hrsg.): Handbuch Marktforschung, 1. Auflage, Gabler, 1999, S. 861–910.

[15] The term "recall" refers to the degree to which a potential consumer remembers a brand or advertising message, cf.: Esch, F.-R.: Werbewirkungsforschung. In: Herrmann, A./Homburg, C. (Hrsg.): Handbuch Marktforschung, 1. Auflage, Gabler, 1999, pp. 861–910.

[16] The term "persuasion" refers to the persuasive power or strength of an advertising message to bring a product, service, or opinion closer to potential consumers.

[17] "...Likeability in brands results in: (1) greater amount of positive association; (2) increased interaction interest; (3) more personified quality; and (4) increased brand contentment", in: https://core.ac.uk/download/pdf/153389217.pdf (retrieved 13/01/2021).

In addition, the above-mentioned pre-test data is often not available in practice in a form in which it can be easily used in the context of campaign controlling, because, e.g.,

- companies may not have conducted these tests with a consistent methodology for the relevant campaigns of the period under review,
- there may often be little variance in the data because the rating scale used is inappropriate (e.g. ordinally scaled characteristics such as "red"—"amber"—"green") or only spots in the top quartile have gone "on air",
- the TV spot might have been further developed after the test (new cut, voice over, etc.) without testing them again,
- the relevant advertising campaigns have possibly not been consistently timed with a start and end time to ensure an accurate determination of the campaign-specific advertising effects.

However, if these points are taken into account and there is sufficient variance and an adequate number of data points, advertising quality can be considered *explicitly* in the marketing mix model. In principle, two approaches can be considered:

1. **Direct (bivariate) analysis of the correlation between pre-test results and the sales impact of a campaign**. Either total scores of the pre-tests or detailed results can be analysed. For example, it could be shown that copies with a persuasion score of over 110 achieve significantly higher sales effects.
2. **Integration of quality copy indicators as additional influencing variable(s) in the multivariate regression model** in addition to the use of all other simultaneously acting and relevant factors such as competitive intensity, weather, promotions, etc.

If, for example, significantly better pre-test values are available for a new advertising campaign, these can be taken into account in any simulation in order to forecast the expected sales success ("What if").

To illustrate this, in Fig. 5.3, the copy test results for selected TV campaigns of a large advertiser are compared with the calculated sales effects of an econometric model (based on the target sales figure).

The expected correlation between pre-test results and sales impact is in general confirmed. But the underlying strategic marketing objective of the campaign must always be considered when evaluating campaigns. In this example, campaign 3 was not focused on sales, but on strengthening the general brand perception. The lack of a sales effect can therefore be explained. However, the extent to which the resulting effects are as expected and what insights can be derived from this for future campaign planning is part of the comprehensive campaign controlling that is about to begin.

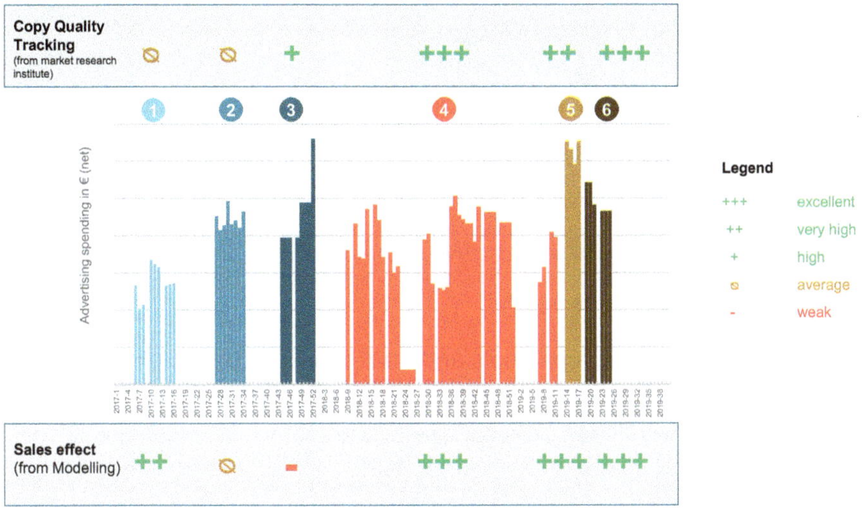

Fig. 5.3 Comparison of copy quality according to market research vs. marketing mix modelling (own illustration)

5.4 Recommendations for Corporate Decision Makers

Marketing budget decisions should always be based on empirically calculated advertising impact. The ROI calculations must take into account the respective campaign strategy. Since the incremental impact can only be validated by econometric modelling, either data science know-how must be built up internally, or an experienced service provider must be called in who ideally offers both—econometric modelling and benchmarking. In addition, it makes sense to consider a powerful software/front-end solution that compares the effects of campaigns on the necessary planning level of the media channels (TV, print, YouTube, Facebook, Google, etc.). Such a tool should also enable budget simulations ("what-if scenarios").

Organisational success factors

Firmly anchor marketing controlling:
Setting up or expanding a marketing controlling team to analyse and simulate advertising campaigns is an important step towards permanently and systematically examining marketing investments and thus contributing to a sustainable increase in ROI. This also ensures that the relevant insights from the campaigns are available at the company itself (and not only at a partner such as the media agency).

Define campaign goals and institutionalise tracking:
The target KPIs of each campaign should already be defined in advance (e.g., image versus sales focus). Continuous analysis of activities in the context of short- and medium-term sales impact and ROI not only per channel but per campaign enables a continuous improvement of strategic marketing.

Make use of data science & business intelligence:
The possibilities of econometrics, intelligent reporting, and a powerful simulation tool should be used for cross-media campaign evaluation. These tools can be developed in-house or provided by third parties.

Methodological / technical success factors

Use econometric models:
A necessary component for determining campaign-specific advertising effects is the use of state-of-the-art models, either with the help of internal experts or through an external service provider. This is the only way to reliably quantify which campaign was economically successful (end-to end). All advertising media should be coded with a start and end time in order to be able to determine specific advertising effects and not just average values for a certain period of time.

Use analytical tools:
It is important to use a powerful solution to support day-to-day operations. This includes populating a benchmarking database for ongoing promotional analysis and planning and simulation of the optimal marketing plan. This allows for increased transparency of historical planning assumptions and easy ex-post analysis and derivation of implications for the coming planning period.

Use pre-test and tracking data in a complementary way:
Structured pre-testing of campaigns along a differentiated scoring scale offers the possibility of benchmarking campaigns in terms of their expected impact even before they are deployed. Ex-post econometric validation of the scores can further improve the validity of the pre-tests if necessary.
In addition, high-frequency advertising trackers with the relevant brand funnel variables are useful to pinpoint the corresponding impact of campaigns on these KPIs.

Modelling, Model Architecture, and Model Quality

6

"Garbage in—garbage out" naturally also applies to analytical marketing optimisation. Therefore, utmost attention should be paid to the selection of the right data (see Chap. 10) as well as to a meaningful validation of the underlying statistical models. Marketing decision makers have to also ask their service providers the right questions for this purpose.

6.1 The Right Target Variable

The aim of econometric models is to isolate and measure the **interdependencies between predictors (influencing factors or drivers) and economic targets (dependent variable, e.g., market share, number of sales units, contracts, or marketing leads)**.

First of all, the selection of a suitable target variable plays an important role: the target variable should be sufficiently close to the marketing impulse and have a sufficiently concrete relationship to commercial success (e.g. sales instead of brand awareness).

Deciding on the "right" target variable is easier in the FMCG sector than in many other industries, as representative and reliable retail panel data is available in most European countries to measure one's own and the competitor's sales and price levels.

In other industries, such as automotive,[1] financial services, or telecommunications, this is more difficult. In the insurance industry, for example, leads (i.e. insurance applications) are often a better target figure because, due to legal requirements and organisational guidelines, the contact or contract process has a

[1]Example: The decision to use the number of hits on the car configurator at Automotive, for example, is a good compromise, as indeterminable external factors such as dealer influence, closing behaviour, and other distorting factors "neutralise" the actual marketing influence.

S. Stürze et al., *Agile Marketing Performance Management*, Management for Professionals, https://doi.org/10.1007/978-3-658-38053-3_6

strong influence on the further course of events up to the conclusion of the contract (or policy) and distorts the original marketing effect.

6.2 The Right Model Architecture

But why do you need a statistical model at all? In short: Because in reality everything happens at the same time and everything has a simultaneous effect on the target variable. The predictors form a network of relationships in which the individual forces interact permanently and dynamically. Every modification can lead to a change in the network of relationships (strengthening or a weakening of forces, overlapping or compensating effects, etc.), both in the case of short-term (e.g. on price, promotions, or competitor behaviour) and long-term (e.g. on brand strength) influencing factors.

Figure 6.1 illustrates this problem: Is the peak in sales in the marked area due to the higher media investment, the stronger promotional activity, the slightly lower price, or a combination of these factors?

This can only be sorted out by a multi-variate model with a high predictive quality.

The above diagram is a simplification of the actual situation. In reality, this network of relationships would have to be expanded by a multitude of further factors (e.g. the separation of media into relevant channels). A good impact model should also take into account the specifics of individual marketing campaigns, as each campaign block and each marketing measure can have a different impact depending on, among other things, copy quality, reach, competitor behaviour, expenditure level, and timing (see Chap. 5).

Furthermore, the media contribution is only one component in the overall relationship structure. In detail, the impact contributions of price, promotions, or distribution effects are no less complex—especially if the activities of competitors

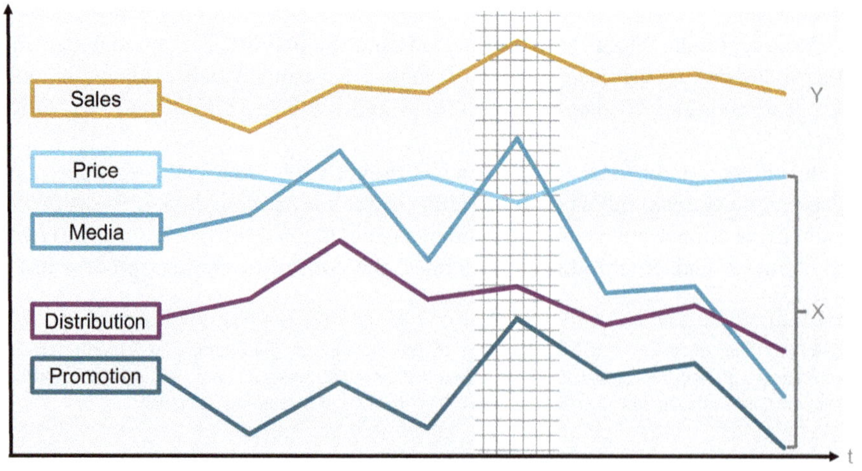

Fig. 6.1 Influence of different impact factors on sales (own illustration)

are also included (e.g. total promotion distribution, price reduction, display, or flyers).

But which influencing factors should be included in an econometric model? In view of the multitude of possibilities, the marketers of a company should discuss the relevant influencing factors (e.g. campaign equipment, media mix, POS promotions) as well as prevailing **hypotheses on the sales impact in close cooperation with modelling experts in a workshop and initially develop a purely qualitative driver tree** (an example is shown in Fig. 6.2). Experience has shown that this approach works across all sectors and is a very sensible way

- to "frame" the project together and make the drivers of sales transparent and—through the participation of relevant experts
- to avoid ending up with a "black box" that no one believes in.

For the data scientists, this approach also offers the opportunity to investigate interrelationships on the basis of hypotheses. The network of relationships identified in the workshop provides the opportunity to formulate the necessary data requirements and to focus on core data.

Based on this understanding of drivers, statistical methods are applied to derive the influence of the drivers on the target variable (Y) 100% quantitatively on the basis of historical data. Figure 6.3 illustrates the influence of the predictors (X = influencing factors) on sales (Y = target = volume/sales) including the illustration of the long-term brand effect (see Chap. 3).

In more complex distribution or market structures, **several models per market/ country are useful to better reflect the business reality**. Let us take the example of an insurance company with a growing online direct business. Here it makes sense to separate the effect of marketing activities on the number of leads, depending on whether they were generated via the online channel or via traditional channels such as brokers. By separating the two, a more precise assessment of the impacting factors can be made. So, the insurance company would run two models for each product group.

The same approach ("divide & conquer") is recommended for providers with strong regional differences (e.g. strong regional beer brands vs. national brands). Thus, for example, it can be quantitatively tested to which extent the effectiveness of marketing measures differs in areas with high or low market shares.

Even if the introduction of sub-models does increase the total number of models considered, the above-mentioned gain in decision support can be considerable. And since the underlying data is often the same, the additional effort is marginal. In any case, it is important to collect and store the data consistently with the relevant subdivisions (regional, channel-specific, etc.).

Granularity of the data and the amount of the available history are also decisive in order to achieve high model quality. Granularity refers to the temporal availability (=resolution) of all impact factors. For a reliable model, this means that all data should be available with at least a weekly resolution. While data from online marketing and sales data is often available to the day, many other factors

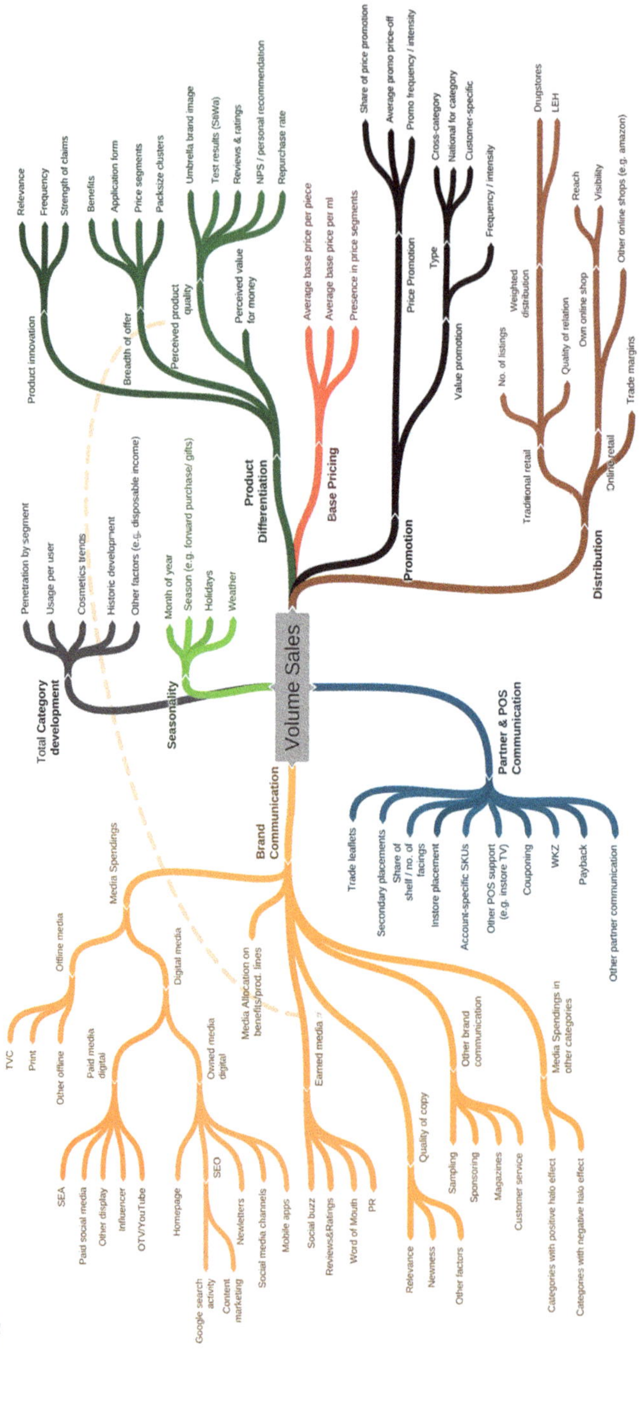

Fig. 6.2 Qualitative driver tree as a result of a hypothesis workshop (own illustration)

Fig. 6.3 Conceptual basic model for determining the sales effect (own illustration)

(e.g. competitor spending or prices) are not. Thus, experience shows that weekly granularity is often the best compromise between achieving accuracy and nodding to realistic data availability.

In order to be able to clearly recognise the patterns of effect correlations from past data, at least 2 years of complete data history are usually necessary, but 3 or 4 years are recommended. Only in this way can seasonal effects and long-term marketing effects be quantified with reasonable precision via brand effects (see also Chap. 10 for data requirements and corresponding best practices).

6.3 Model Quality Is More Than R^2

Ideally, the chosen model architecture should lead to a **high explanatory value**, accompanied by a baseline that is as low as possible. The baseline of a statistical model is the part of the sales volume (or number of leads, contracts, etc.) that cannot be broken down further by the selected predictors. The goal of statistical analysis is therefore to minimise the baseline with the right set of predictors. A low baseline usually indicates a good decision support model. The "weakness" of classic marketing mix models in the past was often their high baseline[2] and the fact that only a limited part of the variance is explained by the selected impact factors.

The **inclusion of more detailed data** (expenditure on all relevant media channels instead of total media expenditure), non-media variables (e.g. coupons, events, number of branches, etc.), but also the long-term effect of investments in the brand (see Chap. 3) helps here to significantly reduce the baseline proportion and improve the forecasting quality.

[2] In statistics, the baseline (e.g. the baseline sales of a company) describes the unexplained share of the total effect. Using the example of the total sales of a company, this is the part that cannot be explained by the impact factors such as media or POS. Other factors that are not included in the model or for which there is no data explain this part.

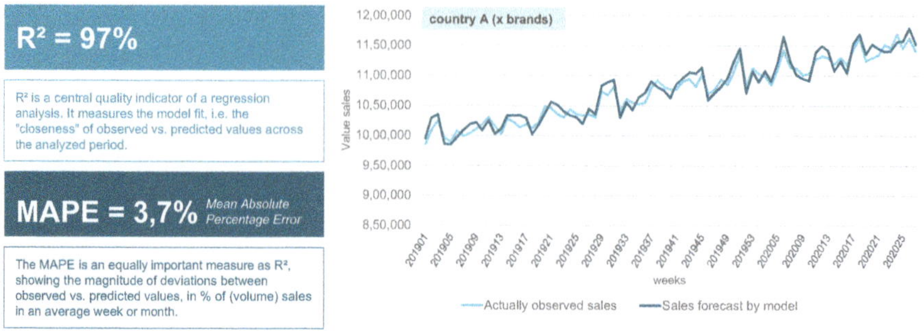

Fig. 6.4 Quality indicators for econometric models (own illustration)

The latter is particularly important from a business point of view, as a statistical model should not only help to explain the past but above all provide decision-making support for the future, based on robust predictions. Therefore, the predictive quality of a model is just as important as its explanatory contribution. **The prediction quality is mainly measured with the help of the Mean Absolute Percentage Error (MAPE).**

This is the "hardest" currency in the field of modelling, namely the forecasting quality—i.e.: how well is the model able to forecast sales (or leads) when it only the influencing factors are available?

In Fig. 6.4, a real modelling example is shown which has a very high explanatory contribution of 97% (R^2). The prediction error of 3.7% for weekly values is very low, i.e., if the model predicts 100 contracts or sales units for any given week, then the true value is very likely to lie in the range between 96.3 and 103.7 contracts.

Of course, a high model quality with a correspondingly low MAPE also depends on the data availability and quality as well as the product category. Therefore, the importance of the driver workshop described above should be mentioned again at this point. Here, the relevant data is collected in a focused manner and discussed with regard to their possible impact influences. Data sources that are only developed or available later can be added in the further course of the process in a model update and thus contribute to a continuous improvement of the model quality criteria.

6.4 The Right Frequency of Updates

For planning reasons, it is important to use data that is as up-to-date as possible. However, what applies to data does not necessarily apply to statistical models. As a rule, these models—especially the advertising elasticities of established media channels (e.g. TV, print, billboard advertising)—are relatively stable over longer periods of time and suitable for strategic allocation analyses.

Therefore, it is important to distinguish three concepts in terms of model updates from a marketer perspective:

- **Data refresh:** Only updated input data is loaded into the database and the reporting platform. Neither the model structure nor the model coefficients (i.e. the influence of the factors) change, but the sales forecasts are kept accurate. This is typically done at a rate of once per month.

- **Recalibration:** New input data (e.g. last month's sales figures and net spend) are loaded into the model and the models are updated with the new data. The model structure remains the same, but the coefficients may change (e.g. the impact of online video over time may be slightly higher). This also results in changed recommendations for the optimal marketing mix. Recalibration can be largely automated and should be done either monthly or quarterly.
- **Remodelling:** For longer intervals (e.g. once every 12 months), the model structure should also be reviewed and, if necessary, adapted to new requirements. A typical example would be the inclusion of a new media channel that has not been previously used or for which no historical data was previously available. Or a division into sub-models is made because online sales have reached a critical size and are to be modelled separately.

In any case, models with high model and prediction quality are recommended in order to exploit the full potential of these statistical approaches. Only then will the quality of the marketing activities be measured cleanly and accurately. Marketers and modellers should decide together on the frequency of updating, e.g., to avoid overdriving old and new channels. The inclusion of new channels should take place right away in order to support the digital transformation with a powerful tool and for the company to be able to see the "bigger picture".

6.5 Recommendations for Corporate Decision Makers

In addition to the appropriate statistical method and corresponding data (see Chap. 10), modelling also requires the following: Knowledge about which factors influence sales and hypotheses about the interdependencies. The following concrete steps are recommended:

Organisational success factors

Driver workshop as integral part of a modelling project:
This should kick-off every modelling project! The immediate result of this workshop is the collection of the main factors influencing the target value ("What influences our sales?") in the form of a driver tree. As a side effect, the same exercise helps to systematically understand data availabilities and needs.

Data collection:
Data on the target and all relevant influencing factors should be available at least in weekly resolution. Both internal systems and external data suppliers should be aligned accordingly. Clear responsibilities are also important: Who is responsible for which data sources, how often is the data updated, where and in what form is it stored? A central database is ideal to enable efficient updating of econometric models. But this is less a technical issue...

Methodological / technical success factors

Selection of the right target variable:
The target variable should be as close as possible to the marketing impulse (i.e., there should be a clear temporal and content-related connection between marketing activities and target variable), as well as having a direct link to the economic success of the company (e.g., leads instead of brand awareness).

Inclusion of all relevant influencing factors:
Ideally, the entire network of relationships (see driver workshop) should also be mapped as completely as possible with quantitative data. This often requires creativity and persistence but is important for a reduction of the unexplained baseline.

Granular data and sufficient history:
Data should be available on weekly level and for the last two to four years. It is important that the underlying definitions are consistent (e.g., regarding product allocation or target groups). This is often referred to as taxonomy.

Consider splitting into sub-models:
The informative value and practical applicability of the findings can often be highly increased by splitting them into sub-models (e.g., for regions or sales channels).

Look at the right quality criteria:
More important than a rigid focus on classical quality criteria such as the coefficient of determination is to ensure that there is a high predictive quality (e.g., low MAPE).

Regular updates:
In a dynamic environment, marketing models also need to be updated regularly. Largely automated monthly or quarterly recalibrations and an annual review of the model structure are advisable.

Multi-touch Attribution and Unified Measurement

7

In the previous chapters, marketing mix modelling (MMM) was discussed in detail as a tool for optimised budget allocation in marketing. In companies that rely primarily on digital marketing channels (SEA, social media, display ads, etc.), however, multi-touch attribution (MTA)—or synonymously attribution modelling—has been established as the method of choice. In this chapter, we not only want to clarify the terminology and the differences, but also provide decision support and recommendations to get the best of both worlds.

7.1 Two Tools: One Goal

Because marketing mix models have a much longer history, they are sometimes considered as somewhat old school, especially by digital marketing experts. Therefore, perhaps the most important aspect of the chapter should be highlighted first:

In principle, MMM and MTA pursue the same goal: quantify the contribution to overall financial success of individual marketing activities as accurately as possible to support an efficient allocation of budgets.

The most relevant difference between the two is their respective lens on the problem:

- Key purpose of **MMMs is to break down the aggregated, i.e. the total value of a performance variable (e.g. sales volume per week) into the (potential) influencing factors** (e.g. media intensity, but also weather, price changes, etc.) and to determine their relative contribution (see Chap. 6). They also offer the possibility of effectively including the long-term brand effects of advertising. Appropriate statistical methods are always used for this purpose, such as advanced regression models. We are writing "potential" in brackets because it is the task of the model to clarify whether an assumed influencing factor really influences sales or not.

S. Stürze et al., *Agile Marketing Performance Management*, Management for Professionals, https://doi.org/10.1007/978-3-658-38053-3_7

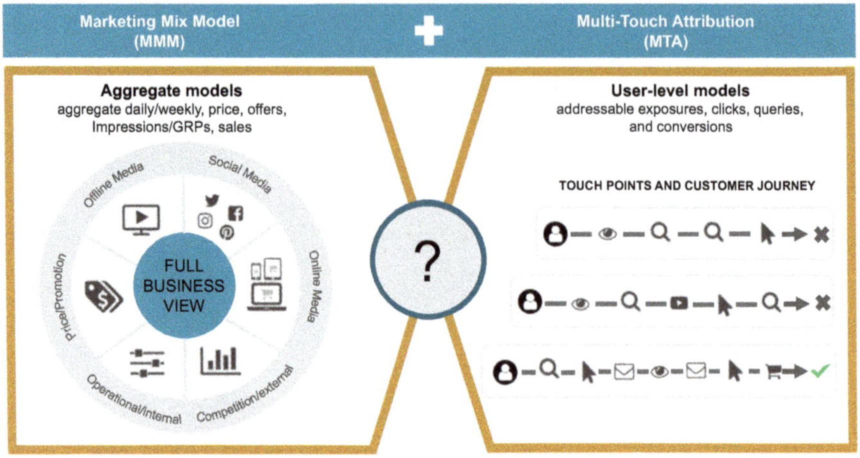

Fig. 7.1 Differences between MMM and MTA (translated from The Drum)

- **MTAs, on the other hand, take the viewpoint of the individual customer journey** and are therefore based on individual rather than aggregated data. They attempt to trace all touchpoints of a customer or lead from the first click on a display banner to the completion of a transaction in the store. In this way, the generated turnover or the gross margin of a single purchase act can be distributed among the preceding impulses or touchpoints with the customer. This distribution can be done with statistical methods, but it can also be based on assumptions, which we will discuss below.

Figure 7.1[1] illustrates these differences again: Both methods—MMM & MTA—serve to determine an impact contribution for as many marketing activities as possible and to use this knowledge in order to then allocate a budget.

7.2 There Is No Such Thing as a Free Lunch: Differences and Use Cases

Despite having the same purpose, there are considerable differences between MMM and MTA due to the different angle for viewing the problem and because of MTA's heritage in digital marketing. These differences yield higher or lower suitability depending on the key questions to be answered. The following table summarises the main differences between MMM and MTA along multiple dimensions:

[1] https://www.thedrum.com/industryinsights/2018/11/28/combined-forces-when-attribution-falls%2D%2Dshort-take-unified-view (retrieved 13/01/2021).

		MMM	MTA
Model	Model used	Statistical model	Often based on attribution *rules* [a]
	Model update	One-time setup, re-calibration as as required	In principle daily with each new transaction
Data	Granularity of the data	Aggregated (e.g., sum of weekly expenditure and sales)	Single customer
	Data source(s)	Existing sources (partly in silos) such as media outputs, CRM, ERP	Cookies & Tags
	Required data volumes	Two to three years history (aggregated weekly data)	As many impressions and per week at the individual individual customer level
Applica-tion	Media channels	All, for which data are available	Mostly digital only [b]
	Mapping new (digital) channels	Requires several months relevant spending	Comparatively fast
	Other marketing and sales activities ("beyond media")	Yes, provided that data available	no
	Other influencing factors (e.g., weather, competition)	Yes, provided that data available	no
	Sales effect	Offline and online	Online only (purchase file must be linked to journey) [c]
	Long-term effect of marketing	Yes, if brand tracking is included	Not possible
	Insights into customer groups / customer segments	Only if data and modelling per customer group are available	Easier possible, theoretically down to the individual customer level

[a]One exception is "Algorithmic Attribution", see the next subchapter on this topic

[b]With the increase in digitalisation of offline channels (keyword "addressable TV"), even traditional channels are gradually becoming assignable to the individual customer

[c]Offline purchase records can be associated with an online journey using tools such as personalised loyalty cards

The colour coding in the table indicates what MMM and MTA are each preferably suited for and where their respective limitations lie:

- MMMs are designed to isolate all influencing factors (not only the actions of the advertiser but also external factors) on an economic target variable such as weekly sales. This can include long-term effects of marketing (e.g. by building brand

loyalty) as well as the influence of non-digital channels such as out-of-home advertising.
- MTAs, on the other hand, are good at breaking down successful customer conversions into individual touchpoints based on individual chains of events. Provided the software systems involved can do this, MTAs allow for a daily update of the relevant insights, as new purchase transactions are generated every day.

Ultimately, it is all about **data** again—**both methods need it, albeit differently in scope:**

- MMMs cannot do without a certain history of at least 2 years of training data for the initial set-up. To explain the variance in the target variable well, it is often necessary to pull together historical data from different "silos" (i.e. from different systems and sources with different responsibilities and taxonomies). Agency changes and the like often complicate this process.
- An e-commerce start-up, on the other hand, which opens an online shop today, can in principle work with MTA from day one. The prerequisite is that all the customer touchpoints and the online shop itself are consistently equipped with the so-called tags (small snippets of code). This is needed to accurately map the journey prior to each transaction and to correctly assign it to the transaction. In established organisations or for offline sales channels, this is by no means a trivial task.
- The fact that MTAs are based on individual (online) data and therefore in many cases require user consent is an increasing challenge, especially in Europe, in view of data protection requirements.

If fewer and fewer users allow cookies to be set, browser settings prevent this, and stricter rules apply regarding the "retention periods"—i.e., ultimately the longevity—of cookies, this may gradually lead to a decline in the applicability of MTAs. Some experts speak of a rebirth of MMMs in this context because they are not dependent on these types of data.[2] We will cover these privacy aspects in more detail in Chap. 8.

7.3 MTAs Are (Too) Often Nothing More Than Rules

Despite the above-mentioned limitations, most e-commerce companies today use one attribution model or another to allocate their marketing budgets between different marketing channels, especially digital ones. The term model can be misleading,

---

[2] Mayer, L.-A., Die Folgen der Cookiekalypse—Warum Marketing-Mix-Modelling jetzt ein Comeback feiert, https://www.horizont.net/tech/kommentare/die-folgen-der-cookiekalypse-warummarketing-mix-modelling-jetzt-ein-comeback-feiert-180991 (retrieved 13/01/2021).

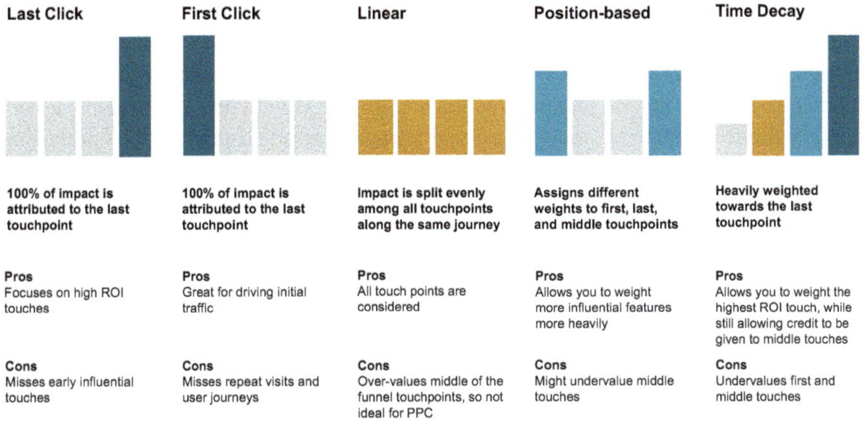

Fig. 7.2 Alternative attribution rules (translated from Crawford, T.: How to Pick the Right Attribution Model for Your Business, retrieved on 13/02/2021 from https://heap.io/blog/right-attribution-model)

however, because in most cases it does not refer to a statistical model as in MMMs. Instead, **an attribution "model" is usually simply a decision for one rule or another**, which then determines to which channels more or less sales impact is attributed.

Two commonly used rules are:

- **Last Click:** 100% of the generated revenue or gross margin of a purchase in the online shop for customer X is attributed to the last interaction (e.g. a click on a Google ad). All other interactions before this are considered ineffective for this specific journey.
- **Position-based ("bathtub"):** 50% of the marketing success is attributed to the first interaction (first click) and 50% to the last (last click).

Figure 7.2 illustrates these two alongside other common attribution rules as well as the implicit assumptions behind them using the example of a customer journey with four touchpoints:

If the selected attribution rule is applied to each and every single customer journey that has been tracked, then the sum of all transactions over a certain period of time yields the impact contribution of each channel for the total business. However, marketing decision makers must be aware that this insight is based on the application of a rule that they themselves have set in advance and which implies corresponding assumptions about the world (see Fig. 7.2).

Newer developments (known as algorithmic attribution) try to compensate for this weakness. In principle, the goal is to determine the attribution rule that best explains the historical behaviour of customers by analysing many historical purchase acts and the corresponding journeys that precede them. This rule can also be specific to certain customer segments and may change over time.[3] Since algorithmic attribution is based on machine learning methods (e.g. neural networks), it requires a very large volume of data (i.e. many observed purchase acts and many clicks preceding these) to derive the correct attribution logic. It is therefore mainly the domain of large e-commerce companies such as Amazon and Zalando, which have a correspondingly large learning sample at their disposal.

7.4 Best of Both Worlds?

The previous explanations have shown that MMMs and MTAs have their respective strengths and weaknesses and thus rightfully coexist. In particular, for CMOs with larger brand portfolios and omnichannel sales there is no viable alternative to MMMs to achieve a truly objective budget optimisation offline and online, which incorporates the long-term development of the brands. At the same time, the use of digital and highly targetable marketing channels is increasing (see Chap. 8), and marketers understandably do not want to forego the level of detail and automation of an MTA.

Multi-channel companies with a mix of online and offline marketing (especially with a high TV share for brand building) chose to increasingly follow an integrative approach that tries to combine the best of both worlds:

- An MMM is used to identify all relevant influences and interdependencies regarding an economic target value. Ideally, this includes short- and long-term effects as well as effects that the company itself cannot influence (e.g. marketing intensity of the competition). **Allocation decisions on a strategic and tactical level are derived from this**, e.g., "*3.8% of the total budget as the optimal spending level for SEA Brand in the month of July for product group X of brand Y*".
- An MTA is used for the fine-tuning of the digital channels and allows for almost real-time adjustment down to the level of the individual customer. **However, this fine-tuning is within the budget guard rails set by the MMM ("single source of truth").**
- A/B testing—i.e., structured experiments—is another essential component of the toolbox, because there will always be channels for which there is no historical data at all and whose effectiveness must first be evaluated through systematic A/B tests. **This has the pleasant side effect that historical data is generated, which helps the MMM and MTA layers to adjust their recommendations over time.**

[3]Haleua, C.: Algorithmic Attribution: Choosing the Attribution Model That's Right for Your Company, https://blog.adobe.com/en/2017/01/12/algorithmic-attribution-choosing-attribution-model-thats-right-company.html#gs.hvlkey (retrieved 13/01/2021).

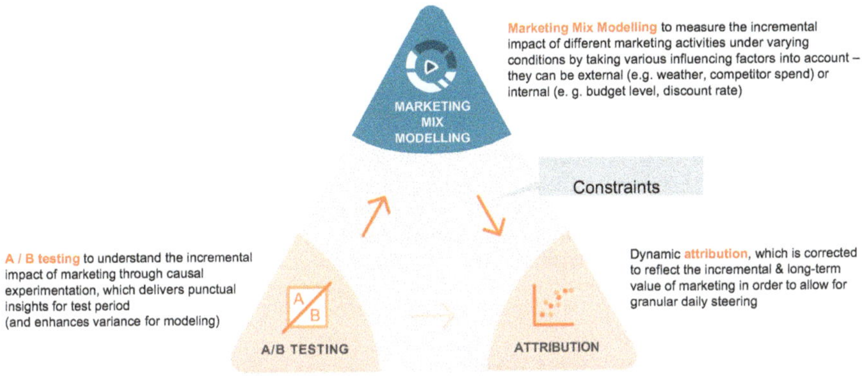

Fig. 7.3 Interplay MMM, MTA, and A/B tests (translated from Stern 2019)

Along these lines, the smart combination of the three tools becomes a kind of flywheel which, when applied continuously and rigorously, leads to ever better allocation decisions (cf. Fig. 7.3).[4]

7.5 Recommendations for Corporate Decision Makers

Certainly, all companies that advertise strive for a solid attribution—i.e. the correct allocation of impact contribution to individual activities. However, as this chapter has shown, there are different ways to do this depending on the data and the objective. How does one make the best of it?

[4] Stern, J.: A framework for ROI-driven portfolio optimisation, In: Conference Proceedings AxCon 2019 (unpublished).

Organisational success factors

Top-down allocation:
In the end, all budgets have the long-term goal of increasing gross profit. Therefore, there needs to be an overarching logic for how budgets are allocated strategically (annual planning) and tactically (e.g., quarters). Ideally, this logic is internationally consistent. It specifies how much budget is allocated to brand X, product line Y, and channel Z in the planning period. The channel managers do the fine tuning (e.g., optimisation of search terms).

Media "vs." Sales Promotions:
The effective allocation also requires that budget planning is done cross-functionally according to clear optimisation criteria (e.g., maximise sales), even if, for example, media and lead acquisition are different departments.

The role of Analytics / Consumer Insights:
These departments should be the drivers of the process and owners of tools and methodologies. They ensure that e.g. A/B tests are coordinated in such a way that they deliver meaningful results and fertilise the next MMM round with their data.

Methodological / technical success factors

Best of Breed:
Our experience is that a best-of-breed approach of MMM, MTA and A/B testing with the appropriate tools for each is a better way to go than searching for the holy grail of "unified measurement" from one source that often disappoints.

Simple interfaces:
The reason for this is also that the (data) interfaces between these tools are actually relatively easy to manage. Example: "MMM sets the budget guard rails for MTA". It just has to be clear which system is in the lead for what.

Don't neglect the power of natural experiments:
You will always have new channels and new products for which there is no historical data. Therefore, cleanly structured tests must be and remain an essential part of the mix. No model can replace this.

Individual Targeting and Privacy 8

In Chap. 4, we discussed the sizeable amounts of investment that are being directed towards digital marketing and the share that is individually targeted.

In the previous chapter, we looked at multi-touch attribution (MTA) as a possible basis for optimising budget allocation in marketing to channels or touchpoints. As described, MTA is based on a database of individual customer journeys, i.e. the knowledge of which clicks and page views preceded each individual purchase act.

These concepts are harbingers of **a marketing reality tailored to individuals, consisting of individual targeting and an individual tracking of consumer responses**. In this chapter, we will look more specifically at the opportunities, risks, and more recent limitations of these possibilities due to legal requirements and recent market dynamics.

8.1 Segment-of-One

In technical terms, individual marketing (or one-to-one marketing) describes the extreme form of customer segmentation with a segment size of 1. Hence, the alternative term segment-of-one marketing:

> 1:1 marketing aims to provide customised offers through individual customer care and customer understanding, which are then able to fulfil the wishes and ideas of the individual customer as precisely and comprehensively as possible.[1]

The concept of individualised marketing can be traced back to scientific literature from as early as the late 1980s and beginning of the 1990s, in particular, the seminal

[1]Translated by authors from German original at https://www.absatzwirtschaft.de/markenlexikon/one-to-one-marketing/ (retrieved 28/02/2021).

S. Stürze et al., *Agile Marketing Performance Management*, Management for Professionals, https://doi.org/10.1007/978-3-658-38053-3_8

	ORGANISATIONAL IMPERATIVES		
Approach:	**Mass Marketing**	**Segment Marketing**	**Selling to Segments of One**
Information needs:	limited	periodic	real time
Decision-making:	highly centralised	centralised	decentralised
Organisation:	functional	functional and teams	integrated system
Long-term Planning:	product	product / market	capabilities

Fig. 8.1 Evolution from mass marketing to segment-of-one marketing (Edelman 1989)

work of Richard Tedlow[2] and the well-known paper "Markets of a Single Customer" by Kara & Kaynak.[3]

The following Fig. 8.1 is based on an article by the Boston Consulting Group from 1989[4] and, in addition to the above-mentioned evolution from mass to segment to individual marketing, it already highlights some organisational requirements that individualised marketing entails:

In marketing communication and above all in budget allocation, one-to-one marketing goes hand in hand with the individual targeting of advertising, i.e. the targeting of individual consumers to maximise the probability of a positive response.

In this context, different forms of targeting—especially in the digital sector—must be distinguished.[5] Two dimensions are particularly relevant for the purposes of this chapter:

- **Anonymity:** Is the consumer to be targeted known by name or not? In the latter case, a distinction must be made as to whether he/she is at least clearly identifiable, i.e., for example, whether it can be said with certainty that the same unique consumer will re-enter an online shop after a few days, even if he/she is not yet a registered customer.
- **Data used:** How broad is the range of attributes relating to an individual consumer that the advertiser can use for the purpose of targeting?
  - If, for example, you consider placing a TV ad just before the news, you can only use the TV channel's media data as a data source, which describe the typical viewers of the programme in terms of their number, socio-demographics, etc.
  - If, on the other hand, you send personalised email newsletters to existing customers of your online shop, in an extreme case a segment-of-one newsletter

[2]Tedlow, R.A.: New and Improved: The Story of Mass Marketing in America, Basic Books, 1990; and: Tedlow, R.A./Jones, G.: The Rise and Fall of Mass Marketing, Routledge, 1993.

[3]Kara, A./Kaynak, E.: Markets of a Single Customer: Exploiting Conceptual Developments in Market Segmentation, In: European Journal of Marketing, Vol. 31(11/12), 1997, pp. 873–885.

[4]Edelman, D.: Segment-of-One Marketing, https://www.bcg.com/publications/1989/strategy-segment-of-one-marketing (retrieved 28/02/2021).

[5]O.A.: Targeting, https://www.onlinemarketing-praxis.de/glossar/targeting (retrieved 28/02/2021).

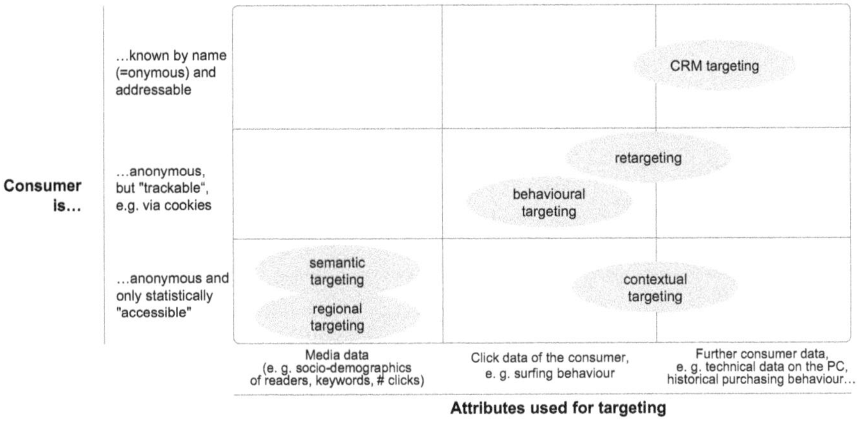

Fig. 8.2 Typical targeting techniques (own illustration)

would be conceivable, which is geared to the individual recipient in terms of design and content and has "learned" about the recipient from the entire stock of data available (historical shopping behaviour, socio-demographics, secondary data on the billing address such as the prevailing income level there, etc.).

Figure 8.2 illustrates the best-known targeting techniques based on these two dimensions:

Of course, **the attributes used for targeting do not necessarily have to be in the possession of the advertisers themselves** (= first-party data). Facebook (in this case the second party), for example, offers advertisers a wealth of targeting criteria, which of course only apply if the advertising message is delivered to consumers within the Facebook universe. A selection of these criteria is shown in the ad booking form shown in Fig. 8.3.

8.2 Benefits of Individual Targeting and the Power of First-Party Data

It is a gross oversimplification, but in our modelling work for multinational advertisers we observe two insights time and again:

1. **If short-term sales maximisation is the goal (= performance), then targeted channels always have a higher ROI on average than mass-market advertising such as radio.**
2. **The more individualised the targeting and the broader the database used for this purpose, the higher the effectiveness of the advertising played out.**

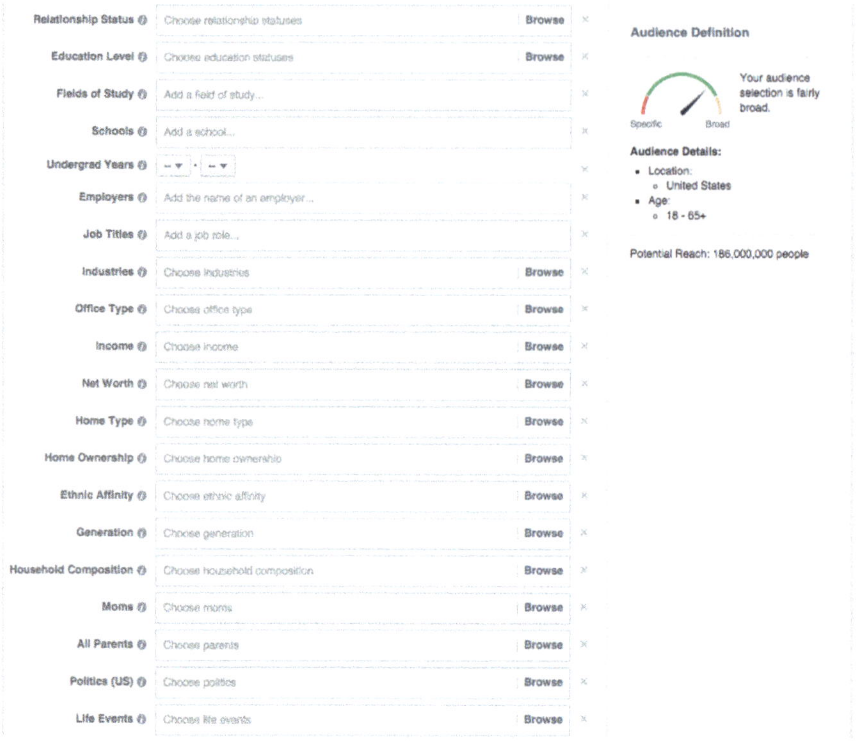

Fig. 8.3 Choice of targeting criteria when booking Facebook ads [https://www.facebook.com/ad_center/create/ad/ (retrieved 18/04/2021)]

For example: Data-driven individualised newsletters are on average more effective than is search engine marketing for relevant keywords.

These two findings are intuitively obvious, as targeted advertising minimises ad waste due to its inherent logic. The second reason for their high effectiveness, however, is that individually targeted forms of advertising such as retargeting or email newsletters are almost always focusing on the lower end of the marketing funnel. In other words, these forms of advertising tend to address customers who already know the advertiser's brand or even—as with retargeting—have articulated interest in certain products in the online shop through their prior click behaviour.

The following practical example of a European retailer with more than 200 physical stores can help to illustrate this: The traditionally most important form of advertising—as with many retail chains—is weekly newspaper inserts in the regions where the retailer has a local presence (= regional targeting). The retailer has allocated more than half of its budget there in the current media mix (cf. Fig. 8.5 below).

For the past 2 years, however, the retailer has also been cooperating with a nationwide loyalty programme and can use this to send out targeted direct mailings

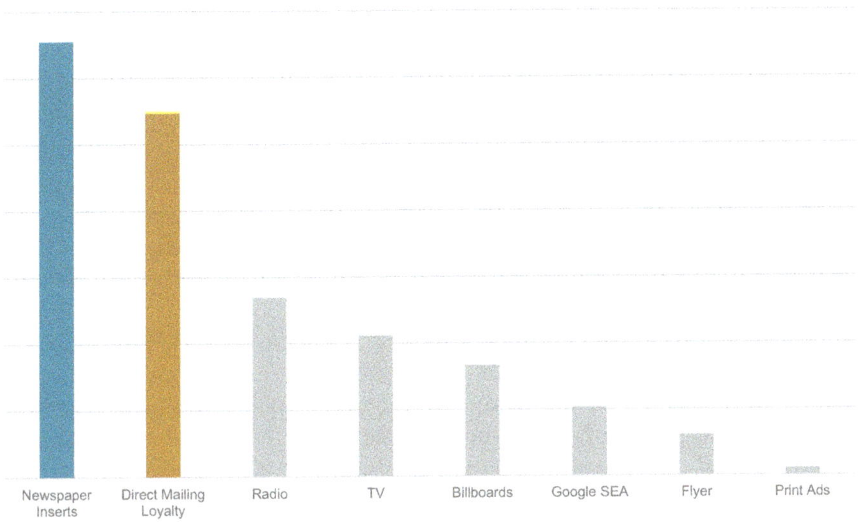

Fig. 8.4 Effectiveness of different media channels at a European retail chain (own illustration)

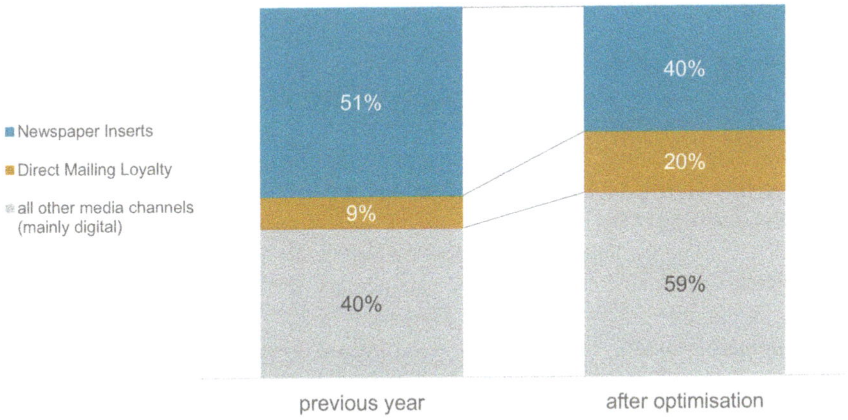

Fig. 8.5 Budget optimisation of a European retail chain derived from modelling (own illustration)

to customers who have recently visited a store (the loyalty card provider has obtained the required opt-ins and sends out the letters on behalf of the retailer).

As a result, this targeted form of advertising achieves an effectiveness (calculated via econometric modelling) that is comparable to that of newspaper inserts—despite a far lower budget of only one-seventh relative to the inserts (cf. Fig. 8.4).

Therefore, in the modelling-based budget optimisation (cf. Fig. 8.5), a significantly higher weighting of this channel is mathematically derived. An even stronger budget allocation to this media channel is currently only limited by the availability of GDPR-compliant addresses.

This example illustrates the **power of first-party data** to drive marketing effectiveness. Whenever advertisers have the opportunity to build their own data pools (contact data and further attributes to improve targeting) about their existing customers and their leads within current legal frameworks, this typically has a short payback period in B2C sectors. The effectiveness of individualised advertising is already high, and targeting one's own customers is more efficient than targeting via third parties such as loyalty card operators or large advertising platforms.

Scientific research confirms these findings: **If targeting based on the user's behaviour is reliably possible, the short-term advertising effectiveness is significantly higher than without it.**[6]

Unfortunately, this does not in the same way and degree apply to publishers, i.e., to the operators of journalistic platforms on the Internet: The presence of cookies and thus the possibility of individual targeting and tracking only offers them a marginal revenue advantage.[7] This could either mean that the bigger share of economic gains from individual targeting stays with the advertisers. Or it means that the targeting possibilities and the reach offered by the big American platforms are channelling most targeted ad spend to them (see Sect. 8.4 below).

8.3 Unmet Expectations and the Risks of Hyper-Targeting

As explained in Sect. 8.1, not all forms of advertising—not even all digital forms—can be individually targeted. Nevertheless, since the first digital banner was displayed in 1994, digital marketing has enjoyed an unprecedented inflow in terms of advertising spending. One important reason for this is the inherent promise of superior effectiveness. And this promise has a lot to do with avoiding wastage through better targeting.

The last 5 years have seen a growing sense of discomfort among the big advertisers, culminating in a famous commentary by Marc Pritchard—CMO of Proctor & Gamble—in the Journal of Marketing in 2021 entitled: "**Half my *digital* advertising is wasted**".[8] His criticism was directed primarily at a "non-transparent, murky, and sometimes even fraudulent digital supply chain". The digital advertising market is dominated by a few big players and there are hardly any independent bodies that measure or control the corresponding KPIs. This leads to systematically overestimated advertising impact and can be illustrated by two examples:

[6]Haan, E./Wiesel, T./Pauwels, K.: The effectiveness of different forms of online advertising for purchase conversion in a multiple-channel attribution framework, In: International Journal of Research in Marketing, Vol. 33(3), 2016, pp. 491–507.

[7]Marotta, V./Vibhanshu, A./Acquisti, A.: Online Tracking and Publishers' Revenues: An Empirical Analysis; Preliminary Draft, https://weis2019.econinfosec.org/wp-content/uploads/sites/6/2019/05/WEIS_2019_paper_38.pdf (retrieved 07/03/2021).

[8]Pritchard, M.: Commentary: Half My Digital Advertising is Wasted ...; In: Journal of Marketing, Vol. 85(1), 2021, pp. 26–29.

- **Ad Fraud/Bots:** Advertisers repeatedly find that switching off their digital advertising media over a certain period of time immensely decreases their website traffic, but there is hardly any difference in sales or revenue.[9] One reason is oftentimes the activity of bots, which "click" on ads. But of course, they do not make any transactions, let alone go to offline shops or feel any long-term brand impact.[10] The initially stellar effectiveness of digital advertising quickly turns out to be a flash in the pan and rightly makes people suspicious of the widespread click-based payment models.
- **Overstatement of reach:** At the beginning of 2021, it became known that Facebook was aware that its targeting tools (see screenshot in Sect. 8.1) in many cases gave a significantly overestimated indication of reach when booking advertising.[11] This is mainly due to the fact that the targeting tools also count inactive accounts in Facebook's user base, which the advertiser also pays for in the case of reach-based payment.

This group of symptoms is all due to the fact that advertisers tend to look at intermediate variables such as reach and clicks when assessing ad effectiveness. The examples show once again how essential it is to concentrate on economic target variables (sales/turnover) instead and to prove the connection between input and economic output by means of econometric models (see Chap. 6).

A second risk of individual targeting is more content-related and is very well described by the following quote from Andrew Willshire:

> Chasing individuals around the internet produces more data than can be managed, yet not enough to solve the problem.[12]

Marketing science often refers to this problem as hyper-targeting:[13] Quasi-individual targeting is of course always feasible or easier to implement if you already have some data on the relevant consumer—or can at least identify him/her with the help of tracking techniques such as cookies.

---

[9] Aral, S.: What Digital Advertising Gets Wrong, https://hbr.org/2021/02/what-digital-advertising-gets-wrong (retrieved 07/03/2021).

[10] Fung, K.: Why Fraudulent Ad Networks Continue to Thrive, https://hbr.org/2015/10/why-fraudulent-ad-networks-continue-to-thrive (retrieved 07/03/2021).

[11] Lomas, N.: Facebook knew for years ad reach estimates were based on, wrong data, but blocked fixes over revenue impact, per court filing, https://techcrunch.com/2021/02/18/facebook-knew-for-years-ad%2D%2Dreach-estimates-were-based-on-wrong-data-but-blocked-fixes-over-revenue-impact-per-court-filing (retrieved 07/03/2021).

[12] Willshire, A.: Attribution is broken, here's how to fix it, https://www.marketingweek.com/digital-attribution-is-broken-heres-how-to-fix-it/ (retrieved 07/03/2021).

[13] Pauwels, K.: Advertisers are too focused on hypertargeting individuals that they have UNDER-invested in awareness, https://www.linkedin.com/posts/prof-dr-koen-pauwels-0789713_unified-marketing-fra-meworkwhen-to-use-which-activity-6757793797658202112-n_Jr/ (retrieved 07/03/2021).

However, this is mainly the case if they are either existing customers or at least relevant leads who have already revealed an interest in certain products or the advertiser's brand through their actions. This can also be the case, for example, if someone has searched for a specific product on a price comparison site. It is a self-fulfilling prophecy that advertising, which targets this "biased" group of people, is almost inevitably more effective.

In the allocation of tight marketing budgets, this might mean that budgets are increasingly concentrated on these seemingly effective forms of advertising—and thus on the 1% of possible consumers—while 99% do not see any advertising: "Advertisers [...] are bombarding the 1% who have bought, and neglecting the 99% who haven't bought yet".[14]

The situation is comparable to the danger of investing all resources in short term, highly effective promotions while disregarding the medium-term health of the brand. Once again, consistent modelling of the advertising impact with consistent inclusion of the medium-term advertising impact (see Chap. 3) offers a way out of the vicious circle as the mid-term danger of hyper-targeting is quantified.

8.4 Limitations Due to Regulation and Walled Gardens

Apart from the challenges of individual targeting described in the previous chapter, the **limitations have increased in recent years due to regulatory activities and market dynamics.**

Firstly, there are efforts of European governments to strengthen the privacy of their citizens in the digital realm.

These efforts culminated in the adoption of the European General Data Protection Regulation (GDPR) in 2018, which brought with it drastic limitations in two key areas:[15]

- Users/customers must explicitly agree to receive individual email newsletters—separately for promotional and non-promotional messages.
- Users/customers must explicitly consent to individual tracking (especially the setting of cookies) on each relevant website. This replaced the previously common opt-out solution.

Another important development also concerns the area of user tracking with cookies, but it was driven rather by the large technology companies themselves than by government intervention. A distinction must be made between first-party

[14] Fou, A.: Digital Marketing Is Like Baseball—Mostly The Catching Part, https://www.forbes.com/sites/augustinefou/2020/09/18/digital-marketing-is-like-baseball-mostly-the-catching-part/?sh=2cca2beb6317 (retrieved 13/02/2021).

[15] Ghosh, D.: How GDPR Will Transform Digital Marketing, https://hbr.org/2018/05/how-gdpr-will-transform-digital-marketing (retrieved 07/03/2021).

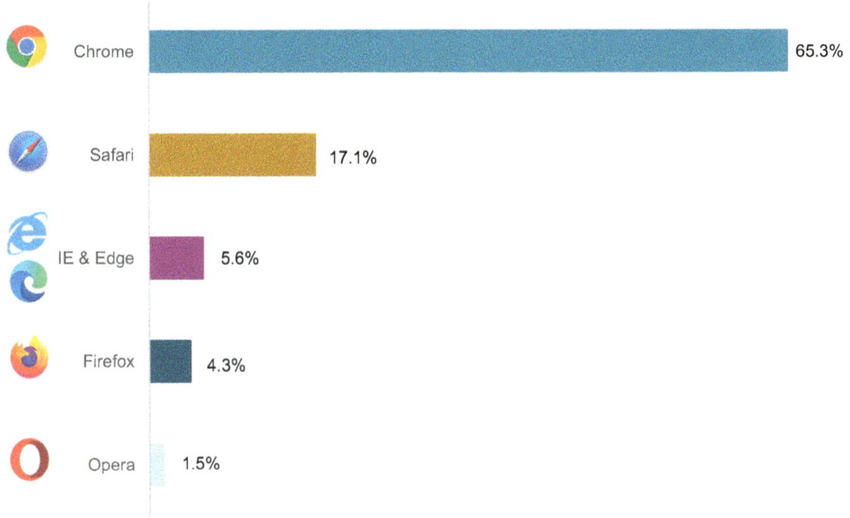

Fig. 8.6 Current browser market shares [own illustration; data from: W3Counter 2021, https://www.w3counter.com/globalstats.php (retrieved 07/03/2021)]

cookies and third-party cookies. The first type is, as an example, stored on consumer devices by online shops visited so that consumers do not have to log in again each time they visit. The latter, on the other hand, are mainly used by marketing agencies (= the third party) to place targeted advertising across websites.[16]

Whether third-party cookies may be stored on the consumer's device depends not only on the user's acceptance (see GDPR) but above all on the web browser. And this market is in turn dominated by a very small number of applications (cf. Fig. 8.6):

Firefox and Opera are generally "privacy-friendly" and therefore have always been very restrictive with regard to individual tracking. Safari (Apple) and IE/Edge (Microsoft) have already been refusing to set third-party cookies in the default setting for several years. Chrome (Google) will do so by the end of 2023. *Ultimately, this means that individual tracking via cookies will only be possible reliably within walled gardens, i.e. the "universes" of the large advertising platforms.*[17] Or, of course, if the advertiser itself possesses first-party data and can thus address consumers directly (see Sect. 8.2). A third possibility is the use of artificial intelligence to determine—without the presence of cookies—, the probability that

[16] O.A.: No need to mourn the death of the third-party cookie, https://thenextweb.com/podium/2020/05/14/no-need-to-mourn-the-death-of-the-third-party-cookie/ (retrieved 07/03/2021).

[17] Hensel, A.: Cookiepocalypse: What the death of the third-party cookie means for retailers, https://www.modernretail.co/platforms/cookiepocalypse-what-the-death-of-the-third-party-cookie-means-for%2D%2Dretailers/ (retrieved 07/03/2021).

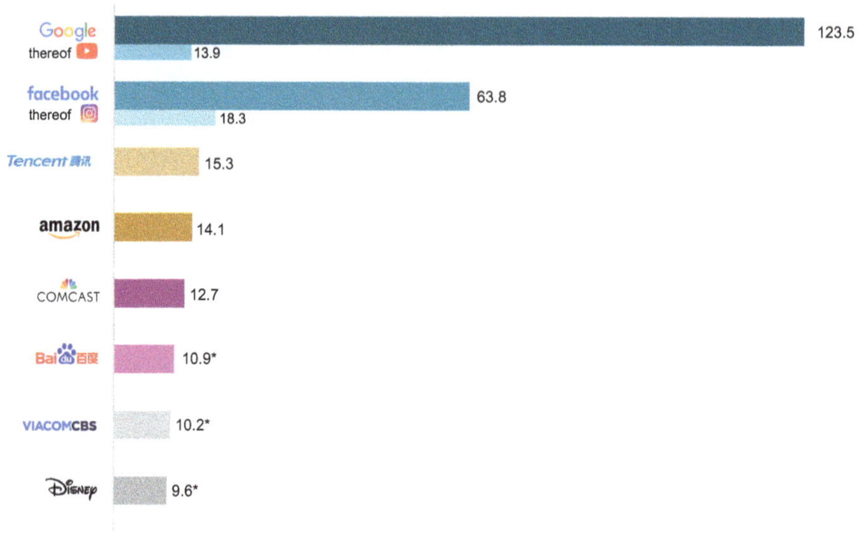

Fig. 8.7 Advertising revenues of the leading digital platforms 2019, in € billion [own illustration; data from Fidler, H.: Google, Facebook, Amazon: Weltgrößte Werbe-budgets gehen längst an Onlineriesen, https://www.derstandard.de/story/2000114492986/google-facebook-amazon-weltgroesste-werbebudgets-gehen-laengst-an-onlineriesen (retrieved 07/03/2021)]

consumer A is the same as B. This is sometimes referred to as "Contextual Targeting 2.0".[18]

Against this backdrop, it will be relevant to observe *how the large Silicon Valley technology platforms reshape their business models around the topic of privacy in the upcoming years*. Figure 8.7 shows the advertising revenues of the tech giants in 2019, which we will discuss individually below:

- *Amazon*—in addition to its e-commerce business—is also becoming an increasingly relevant advertising platform globally: Already in 2019, Amazon has generated more than EUR 14 billion in revenue globally from advertising. In the subsequent 5 years, this figure was expected to rise to over EUR 70 billion. This made Amazon the fastest-growing digital advertising platform in the world.[19] Amazon's attractiveness as an advertising medium is of course primarily due to the power of its first-party data, i.e. the depth of information about the preferences of its over 300 million customers worldwide. This means that Amazon hardly needs any additional data to target these customers very specifically—or to do so on behalf of advertisers.

[18] O.A.: Why AI means the return of contextual targeting, https://www.warc.com/newsandopinion/news/why-ai-means-the-return-of-contextual-targeting/43241 (retrieved 07/03/2021).

[19] Graham, M.: Amazon's ad business will gain the most share this year, according to analyst survey, https://www.cnbc.com/2021/01/12/amazons-ad-business-will-gain-most-share-this-year-analyst-survey.html (retrieved 07/03/2021).

- *Apple* has not always been known as a guardian of its users' privacy. In the 2000s, for example, the iPhone manufacturer—with the help of a unique device ID—allowed app developers and advertisers to uniquely identify users at any time. In more recent history, however, Apple has discovered privacy as a key differentiator for its brand and has taken many technical precautions to make the targeting of its affluent customers more difficult.[20] Such a strategic decision is easy for Apple because the hardware company is not dependent on advertising revenues.
- For *Google*, on the other hand, this does not apply at all (see chart above). Nevertheless, its parent company Alphabet has not only decided to block third-party cookies in its own browser, Chrome, starting from the end of 2023 but to go well beyond that: Even within its own universe (which also includes the online video platform YouTube), there will from then on no longer be any individual tracking of users.

Instead, Google's newer targeting techniques rather offers cohort-based targeting—in effect, targeting based on customer segments.[21]

- With its huge reliance on targeted advertising, *Facebook* could turn out to be the big loser of these trends, especially when it comes to serving ads across its whole ecosystem (Facebook, Instagram and, in the future, WhatsApp), as this will no longer be as easily possible as in the past after the introduction of the innovations announced by Apple and Google are implemented.

8.5 Is Spray'n'Pray Coming Back Now?

In response to the restrictions on individual targeting by regulators and the platforms themselves, *voices are getting louder proclaiming a return to the dark ages of marketing:*

> This echoed other ad-tech types' warnings of a return to a‚spray and p[r]ay' world where, once again, half of all ads are wasted but no one knows which half.[22]

This expresses the fear that a restriction of targeting options is automatically accompanied by an increase in marketing costs due to two effects:

[20] O.A.: Apple's privacy policy kicks Facebook where it hurts, https://www.economist.com/business/2021/02/06/apples-privacy-policy-kicks-facebook-where-it-hurts (retrieved 07/03/2021).

[21] O.A.: FLoC: Google wants to replace third-party cookies with this technology, https://t3n.de/news/ floc-technik-google-third-party-cookies-werbung-personalisiert-targeting-1352751/ (retrieved 07/03/2021).

[22] O.A.: Apple's privacy policy kicks Facebook where it hurts, https://www.economist.com/business/2021/02/06/apples-privacy-policy-kicks-facebook-where-it-hurts (retrieved 07/03/2021).

a) Cost per impression/click in digital marketing increases
b) Reduction of advertising effectiveness due to wastage.

The first fear may well become a reality rather sooner than expected: Recent developments inevitably increase the market power of the big platforms—and thus their influence on pricing. It remains to be seen how the increasing competition from the comparatively new player in the digital advertising landscape—Amazon—will counteract this.

The second point, on the other hand, we consider to be highly exaggerated. We are quite convinced that privacy and marketing effectiveness are not necessarily opposites:

- It is true that targeted digital marketing is—on average—more effective than, for example, advertising on linear television. However, it mainly addresses consumers who have already moved further along the purchase funnel, and it has a rather small brand-building effect (see Chap. 4). It is therefore only one—albeit important—part of the mix. Exaggeration quickly leads to the hyper-targeting described above.
- Individually targeted digital marketing remains possible! Advertisers have always had to pay a price for access to an interesting target group. Whether this is done more efficiently via the large platforms or by building up their own first-party data is up to each CMO to decide.

However, it is also true that individually targeted digital marketing often gives the impression that dynamic budget optimisation in marketing is possible without effort, without own data management (see Chap. 10), and without building analytic skills in-house. One marketing scientist exaggerated this in a personal conversation at a conference as follows:

> Programmatic [advertising] was not designed to help marketers do marketing; it was designed to help ad tech companies make more money off of marketers who like the video-game-like experience of buying ads.

Therefore, the latest privacy developments could even have the interesting and very positive side effect of motivating marketers to focus more on their core competencies such as clean target group definition, brand building incl. the appropriate media mix. And to expand their competencies in the area of modelling and data management. *The marketing mix models described in Chap. 6 manage completely without individual data and therefore will never conflict with GDPR or similar rules at any time. And: They are even able to cross the walls of any walled garden because they explain the relationship between input and commercial output—both are very well known to the advertiser and does not rely on "walled KPIs".*

8.6 Recommendations for Corporate Decision Makers

With regard to individual targeting and segment-of-one marketing, some promises have certainly not been fulfilled and yet the potential of the technologies is huge. Due to the current changes, open eyes are required in the coming years with regard to data protection and the actions of Big Tech. Nevertheless, some basic rules can be derived as follows:

Organisational success factors

Think intensively about building 1st party data pools:
As described above, directly addressing potential customers is often a highly effective channel. Of course, this is more difficult for traditional CPG brands, which are dominantly sold through retailers. But even here, today's world of omnichannel distribution offers exciting opportunities for direct consumer contact in a GDPR-compliant manner.

Don't get carried away by high levels of intermediate KPIs:
Views and clicks go as fast as they come. In addition, they may be generated by non-human actors (bots) who have little interest in the goods or brand messages. Therefore, the focus with regard to the marketing effect always must ultimately lie on financial KPIs.

Methodological / technical success factors

Tend towards MMMs instead of MTAs:
Marketing mix models (see chapters 5 and 6) are based on aggregated data, e.g., advertising spendings and the total # of leads or sales of a week or a day. They do not require sensitive individual data. And they are geared to find general patterns. So, if you want to avoid the risk of hyper-targeting, MMMs tend to be more suitable and are also inherently GDPR-compliant.

Experiments are vital, especially in combination with modelling:
A big advantage of targetable channels is certainly that even with smaller investments you can see relatively quickly whether an effect occurs (as long as this effect is not only measured by the number of clicks - see above). Therefore, companies should not shy away from controlled experiments ("week on, week off"). They have the additional advantage of fertilizing the next round of modelling, as the model can in turn learn from more data and more variance in the data.

Agile Marketing, Agile Budgeting

9

In a constantly dynamically changing environment, even the most advanced optimisation models can only take full effect if they are regularly applied and updated, and also provided this takes place within the framework of an institutionalised process.

9.1 The Basics of Agile Marketing

Marketing agility can be defined in business practice as the "**extent to which an entity rapidly iterates between making sense of the market and executing marketing decisions to adapt to the market**".[1] It is therefore a matter of quickly analysing and understanding newly arising issues and challenges, and reacting to them as quickly as possible by adjusting previously made decisions—if necessary. This all takes place in a regular, iterative process (cf. Fig. 9.1).

Agile marketing organisation manifests itself where the key marketing decisions within a marketing year—supported by processes and tools and based on current data and insights—are continuously (dynamically) scrutinised and adjusted.

In his book "The Speed of Thought", Microsoft founder Bill Gates described more than 20 years ago the possibilities and advantages of digital data streams as well as the monitoring and decision-making processes and implementation possibilities based on them. According to Gates, digitalisation not only leads to an acceleration of the process of measuring and evaluating decisions, but also to a

[1] Kalaignanam, K./Tuli, K.R./Kushwaha, T./Lee, L./Gal, D.: How to Maximise the Potential of Marketing Agility. In: Journal of Marketing Webinar, 2020, https://www.ama.org/2020/10/14/how-to-maximise-the-potential-of-marketing-agility/ (retrieved 13/01/2021).

S. Stürze et al., *Agile Marketing Performance Management*, Management for Professionals, https://doi.org/10.1007/978-3-658-38053-3_9

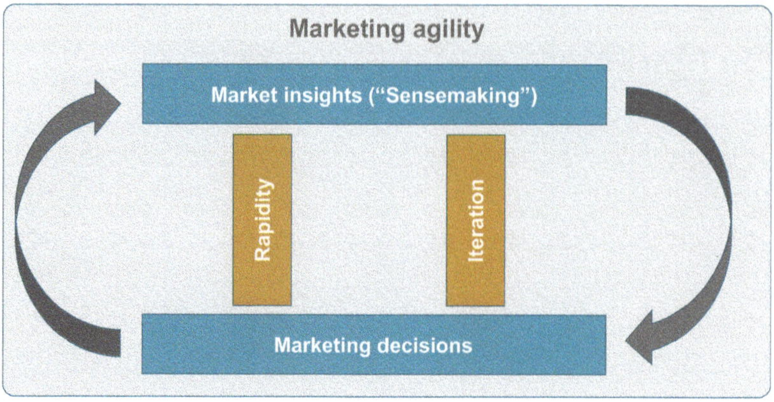

Fig. 9.1 Elements of agility in marketing (adapted from Kalaignanam et al. 2020)

fact-based readjustment. **Regular readjustment is probably the most important building block of agile marketing.**[2]

Just a few years after Gates' book, guiding principles of agile software development were formulated in 2001 in the "Agile Manifesto",[3] on the basis of which the "Agile Marketing Manifesto"[4] was developed in 2012.

9.2 Agile Marketing: The Key to Success?

A 2016 article by the consulting firm McKinsey outlines a number of prerequisites for agile marketing.[5] For example, a marketing organisation should have a **clear vision** of what it wants to achieve with its agile initiative (e.g. which customer segments it wants to attract or which customer decision paths it wants to improve). Also, **sufficient data, analytics, and the right kind of technological infrastructure should be in place**. This infrastructure helps to collect, aggregate, and organise data, to support decisions based on predictive models, and to measure and evaluate the success of the decisions or actions, as well to counter steer if necessary, by making the required adjustments.

[2]Agile management is "an iterative and adaptive process in which small and highly networked teams can produce rapid solutions in simple process cycles and respond directly to feedback from stakeholders." https://www.agilemarketing.net/GettingStartedWithAgileMarke-ting.pdf (retrieved 13/01/2021).

[3]Brandl, M.: Werte und Prinzipien des Agile Marketing Manifesto, http://www.modernmarketer.de/werte-und-prinzipien-agile-marketing-manifesto/ (retrieved 13/01/2021).

[4]https://agilemarketingmanifesto.org/ (retrieved 13/01/2021).

[5]Edelman, D./Heller, J./Spittaels, S.: Agile marketing: A step-by-step guide, https://www.mckinsey.de/business-functions/marketing-and-sales/our-insights/agile-marketing-a-step-by-step-guide# (retrieved 13/01/2021).

Very concretely, agile marketing means, for example, that the placement of a TV advertising campaign is discontinued if the performance factors already indicate low efficiency after the first few weeks. If the current campaign is discontinued, further measures are necessary—the media plan as a whole should be scrutinised. The necessary decisions are made **on the basis of evidence**.

Agile marketing planning thus aims to constantly monitor the effectiveness of the various channels and measures and, if necessary, to trigger a reallocation of resources. It also means that media channels that have delivered weak ROI values in the past should not continue to be targeted without valid justification (e.g. not saying: "We will test three more ideas in this digital channel until the end of the year. Then we will decide again").

The consequence is that agile marketing planning continuously reviews all decisions made with regard to resource use, target achievement, and target adjustments—and modifies them if necessary.

McKinsey partner Aaron De Smet comments that agility has nothing to do with organisational chaos or fickleness, instead it requires a solid, well-structured organisational basis:

"***Agility is not incompatible with stability—quite the contrary. Agility requires stability for most companies.*** *Agility needs two things. One is a dynamic capability, the ability to move fast—speed, nimbleness, responsiveness. And agility requires stability, a stable foundation—a platform, [. . .] of things that don't change. It's this stable backbone that becomes a springboard for the company, an anchor point that doesn't change while a whole bunch of other things are changing constantly.*"[6]

9.3 How to Implement Agile Marketing

Agile marketing and agile budgeting are thus an expression of a corporate decision regarding sustainable marketing investments:

- To **analyse** marketing investments with regard to their goals and profitability (return on marketing) ("What is to be achieved?"),
- To **evaluate** marketing investments ("Which measures proved to be effective?")
- And to **question** marketing investments with regard to their benefit ("With which use of resources can I achieve my goal even better?").

However, agile marketing and agile budgeting require management to collect the necessary **data** regularly and in stable formats, to roll out **tools** with which the central analyses and optimisations can be carried out in a user-friendly way, to incentivise an **agility mindset**, and to anchor corresponding **processes** in the organisation.

[6] See also: https://www.mckinsey.com/business-functions/organization/our-insights/the-keys-to-organizational-agility# (retrieved 13/01/2021).

Data is the "raw material" of any analysis and thus the basis for continuously understanding current developments and drawing consequences from them. In order for this data to be processed and used sufficiently quickly, the relevant information must be available in stable formats, in sufficient **granularity** (at least weekly resolution), in **machine-readable form** (e.g. xls, csv) and **within a short time** (e.g. 4 weeks after the event at the latest). Central data for agile budget planning are, among others:

- Development of the target figure(s) (sales, turnover, leads, new customers, visitors, etc.),
- own offline and online marketing activities (net expenditure, GRPs, impressions, views, mailings/circulation, etc.),
- competitor marketing (e.g. Nielsen Gross Spendings),
- important variables beyond marketing communication (distribution/branch network, price development, promotion intensity, product changes, affiliate activities, etc.),
- central general market information (overall development, new products of the competition, regulatory changes, consumer mobility, etc.), and
- development of brand KPIs (awareness, relevant set, consideration, etc.).

In order to be able to regularly and quickly convert the available data into insights and consequently into decisions, suitable, user-friendly tools are needed. Tools for agile marketing budgeting should possess the following functionalities:

- **Upload portal or fixed data connection:** Data ingestion into the tools should happen within the framework of a clearly defined, efficient process.
- **Automated data transformation:** The above raw data should be merged via automated, script-based routines and processed in predefined analyses.
- **Model updates:** The underlying statistical models, which quantify the impact that the individual marketing activities had on the target variable, should be able to be updated automatically (or with minimal time expenditure) on the basis of the most current data.
- **Budget optimisation:** The budget allocation onto the different channels, activities, and budget units (brands, product categories, countries, etc.) should be subject to algorithm-based optimisation.
- **Flexible constraints:** The optimisation algorithm should be able to work within user-defined constraints, e.g. respecting that a commitment regarding a sponsoring activity has been already made and cannot be cancelled, or that a specific activity cannot be expanded due to external restrictions.
- **Simulation:** "What-if" forecasts based on alternative marketing plans and allocation options should be possible (e.g. "How much more turnover can I generate if I increase my YouTube investments by 50 k EUR?").
- **Reporting and campaign tracking:** Tools for agile marketing should allow easy and user-friendly access to all collected data and visualisation of all relevant

market developments at any time (e.g. "Are the numbers of visitors a reflection of my new marketing campaign?").

Perhaps one of the most important aspects of agile marketing is its ability to instil a **culture and mindset within the organisation** that change and deviation from the previously agreed marketing plan is not a mistake or an admission of error, but the correct and efficient response to changing conditions.

In order to institutionalise agile marketing in the company, **the planning and analysis processes must be adapted accordingly**. This includes at least two aspects:

- **Planning and review processes:** Instead of a classic planning process with lengthy bottom-up and/or top-down communication, we recommend a zero-based budgeting process, supported by systems and complemented by regular, iterative review processes. Only the general framework conditions (e.g. the absolute budget amount, minimum shares for certain channels and brands) are set top-down annually; the monthly adjustments are made at short notice and largely autonomously within the marketing department. In return for this autonomy, the marketing department must be accountable for the efficiency of the measures at any time—which in turn is represented via the above-mentioned tools. Short-term budget adjustments can be made quickly, as the decision-maker is directly aware of the expected implications for the target figure.
- **Data processes:** To support these planning processes, a focused collection and preparation of success-critical data is carried out with clearly predefined formats and KPIs.

If these steps are implemented consistently and are part of an established process instead of just ad hoc initiatives, **this pays off via a sustainable increase in marketing ROI**. McKinsey published the following effects in a comparison of companies with vs. without a systematic approach. Initiatives that are anchored in the organisation through a permanent solution not only show a sustainable development of the potential, but also additional effects through the resulting learning processes (cf. Fig. 9.2).[7]

9.4 Recommendations for Corporate Decision Makers

Those responsible for marketing decisions should focus in particular on the implementation of the above-mentioned organisational and technical factors.

[7] Bauer, T./Freundt, T./Gordon, J./Perrey, J./Spillecke, D.: Marketing Performance. How Marketers Drive Profitable Growth, Wiley, 2016, p. 14.

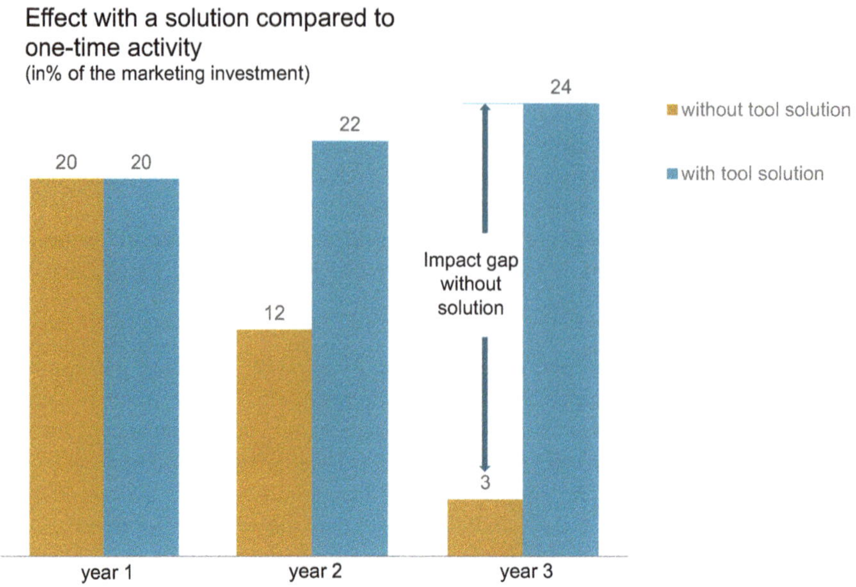

Fig. 9.2 Effect of optimisation measures with vs. without tool solution (translated from Bauer et al. 2016, p. 145)

Organisational success factors

Agile marketing cannot do without data:
Define clear responsibilities, who is accountable for which input data (e.g., who provides the online media data in which rhythm and in which format and how is it further processed?).

Adapt planning processes and question your mindset:
Instead of classic annual or half-year planning, specify only the major "guard rails" for the longer term (budget level, minimum shares for certain channels and brands), while the exact distribution of the budget onto the individual activities is regularly analysed and revised by those responsible, without the need for a marathon of meetings and top management decisions. It is important to note that corrections and adjustments are a central principle of agility and not a mistake or error. Zero-based budgeting is a suitable principle for agile marketing.

Systematic efficiency controlling instead of ad hoc initiatives:
Agile marketing requires that the central target figure for the ongoing evaluation and optimisation of measures has a direct relationship to the economic success of the company (e.g. leads or purchase acts instead of brand awareness), and that marketing is able to measure and report the efficiency of the measures on an ongoing basis and without great effort.

Methodological / technical success factors

Measurement and data collection:
Agile marketing requires a broad, consistent, granular, and up-to-date database. For this purpose, the data that is often available in "silos" (i.e. distributed across different areas and persons responsible) must be integrated in one place. In addition, a fixed data structure must be defined from which no deviation is allowed, because otherwise, no automatic and thus fast and efficient processing of the data is possible.

Testing and rolling out tools:
Agile marketing cannot be implemented today without technical support. This includes both the automatic integration and processing of the latest data and an automated analysis of the information based on suitable econometric models. However, their results and functions must also be retrievable in a form that marketing decision-makers can work with. Appropriate user-friendly tools can either be developed internally by the own data science department, purchased from external service providers, or developed in cooperation.

Digression II: Zero-Based Budgeting (ZBB)—Blessing or Curse?

ZBB does not mean having to swallow a 100% budget cut. The concept originated in the corporate finance departments of larger corporations with many budget allocation units (brands, countries. . .). McKinsey defines it relatively broadly as

> Repeatable process that organizations use to rigorously review every dollar in the annual budget, manage financial performance on a monthly basis, and build a culture of cost management among all employees.[8]

In short, ZBB brings "tabula rasa" to each new planning period. Applied to marketing: The budget allocation for each combination of brand x product line x media channel should be regularly scrutinised in a structured way and justified anew. This can be very time-consuming, but also very worthwhile: between 10 and 25% efficiency increases are possible if the principle is applied consistently in marketing.[9]

Thus, ZBB also has a close link with many of the topics covered in this book:

- **Budget allocation is more than just a media mix** (see Chap. 2): ZBB embodies exactly this principle. Regular scrutiny across the entire "playing field" of budget allocation in marketing—not only with regard to the tactical question of a media mix.
- **Solid, structured** processes (see example in Chap. 2): In larger groups, ZBB brings about the regular, *conscious* review of thousands of budget decisions. This requires structured processes and in our experience is hardly possible without tool support.
- **Agile marketing** (see Chap. 9): The mindset required for ZBB and the tools needed for regular, dynamic budget allocation fortunately overlap with those required for an agile marketing organisation. ZBB and agile marketing are complementary and leverage each other. Thus, ZBB should also be understood as a helpful vehicle for gradually increasing marketing ROI, as it carries the principle of sprints.

(continued)

[8]Callaghan, S./Hawke, K./Mignerey, C.: Five myths (and realities) about zero-based budgeting, https://www.mckinsey.com/business-functions/strategy-and-corporate-finance/our-insights/five-myths-and-realities-about-zero-based-budgeting (retrieved 17/02/2021).

[9]Jacobs, J./Longo, R./Sen, M./Timelin, B: Zero-based productivity—Marketing: Measure, allocate, and invest marketing dollars more effectively, https://www.mckinsey.com/business-functions/operations/our-insights/zero-based-productivity-marketing-measure-allocate-and-invest-marketing-dollars-more%2D%2Deffectively (retrieved 24/03/2021).

- **Marketing elasticities and modelling (see Chap. 6):** For good reasons, ZBB prescribes the consistent justification of budget allocation and the documentation of the rationale for a budget decision. In marketing, this requires at least an approximate knowledge of marketing elasticities—i.e. the effectiveness of advertising for different brands and product lines ("What does an additional dollar mean?"). If one does not know whether advertising works better with brand A or B, one cannot make a well-founded allocation decision. This in turn means that ZBB becomes a more powerful instrument for increasing marketing ROI the more well-founded the underlying models for determining advertising impact are. If relative marketing effectiveness can be empirically determined at the push of a button, ZBB will certainly not be child's play—but it will be much less cumbersome.

Upshot: ZBB is an expense in terms of process excellence, but one that can be verifiably rewarding for the bottom line. However, companies should first gain an understanding of relative marketing effectiveness before changing their budget process—in order to lay a solid foundation for ZBB.

"The Good, The Bad and The Ugly": Data Requirements and Formats for a Successful and Cost-Effective Implementation 10

Data availability and cost-effective data consolidation are often in the spotlight in discussions with service providers, especially for pilot projects. Not infrequently, this element is the great unknown factor in the providers' calculations and can be the largest independent cost block in a PoC.

Furthermore, proactive management of these aspects is a relevant lever in order to ensure a cost-efficient and fast update of models.

While Chap. 9 gives an overview of the relevant implementation elements for an agile and dynamic approach, this chapter focuses on the following questions:

- Which data sources should a good model take into account?
- What are the basic requirements the selected data sources should fulfil?
- What are the differences in the data structure, and what is it that influences the cost-efficient processing of this data in particular?
- How do you deal with countries/brands that have heterogeneous data landscapes? In this context, the question which approaches should be taken for "data-poor" allocation units is often of interest.

10.1 Data Sources and Basic Requirements for Model Variables

In addition to traditional standard data such as retail panels, brand trackers or digital media data, the inclusion of numerous customer-specific data helps to model a realistic representation of the marketing-related effects on the selected success variable (e.g. turnover or volume). Therefore, models that achieve a high forecasting quality usually contain a combination of standard sources and customer-specific data, as shown in Fig. 10.1.

It is essential to ensure a consistent minimum level of granularity for all included data sources. Figure 10.2 lists examples of critical minimum requirements.

S. Stürze et al., *Agile Marketing Performance Management*, Management for Professionals, https://doi.org/10.1007/978-3-658-38053-3_10

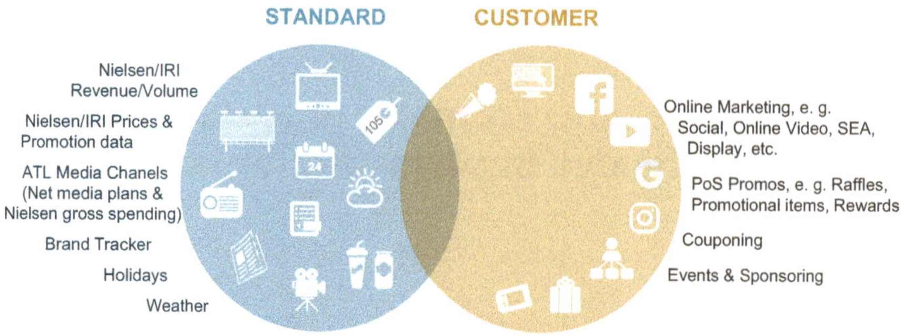

Fig. 10.1 Combination of standard and customised data sources (own illustration)

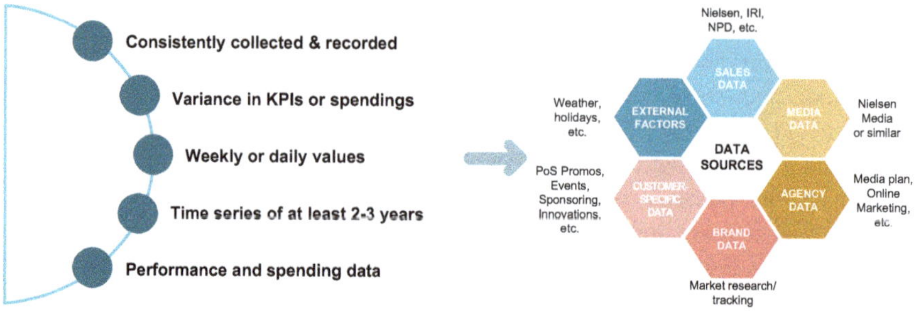

Fig. 10.2 Typical data sources and minimum requirements for history and granularity (own illustration)

In particular, it is vital to have a minimum number of observation points (e.g. 156 data points for 3 years of weekly data) with relevant variance (both in terms of frequency and amplitude).

The underlying requirements are mostly more far-reaching. In the following, we illustrate this using, as an example, data in the area of digital advertising:

- **Required as mandatory:**
  - Table format,
  - Weekly split (totals for Monday to Sunday),
  - Complete period of the model or—alternatively—complete period of existing channel use,
  - Split of media channels in accordance with desired insight gain,
  - Net advertising spend/cost for all channels,
  - Weekly data with relevant variance,
  - SEA split into SEA brand versus generic,
  - Online video (OLV) split into YouTube versus other platforms,
  - YouTube Masthead separated from YouTube video ads,
  - Information on (major) strategic changes in digital marketing/campaigns.

- **Highly recommended:**
  - At least one performance KPI for each channel, recorded consistently over time,
  - YouTube and other OLV split into Skippable vs. Non-Skippable,
  - Split social media channels based on platforms to be optimised (Facebook versus Instagram versus TikTok) or other internal granularity,
  - Split display into classic banner vs. retargeting banner vs. video ads (display video can be equivalent to other OLV in certain cases).

A good external service provider brings similar guidelines in terms of granularity and KPIs for the different data sources and works with the client to continuously enhance the models by improving the data basis (=strategic data management).

10.2 Data Structure: Small Differences with a Big Effect

Suppose the relevant data can be provided to the desired extent. In that case, a central question for data providers (e.g. media agency) and the modeller is in which data format this information is available. Depending on the maintenance of this data at the data provider, one of the two parties often has to make a considerable effort to transform the available information into a usable format before the actual modelling can begin.

The preferred solution is to provide the information in a classic table format in which all information is available in the form of weekly rows. This can be done either in a data matrix across channels (cf. Fig. 10.3) or split up into lines showing channels per week (cf. Fig. 10.4). In the following, this is illustrated using the example of media plan data.

Unfortunately, data sources—especially media plans—are often available in a different form because their purpose is different (e.g. to create an overview for the advertiser). The following Fig. 10.5 is an example of this:

In summary, it remains to be pointed out that it is in the interest of the client/advertiser, in particular, to become actively involved in the process of data collection and templates at an early stage. It is often possible to significantly reduce the time and costs involved and further develop the required data exchange with the relevant agencies going forward. These data templates are also the basis for ensuring consistent reporting by the new partner, e.g. when changing agencies.

10.3 Dealing with "Data-Poor" Allocation Units

As a general rule, comprehensive models should be applied where the associated marginal benefit (turnover and profit size) justifies it. Therefore, many pilots take place in customers' main sales markets, which is something that often correlates with extensive and/or easily accessible data.

				Facebook						Instagram						YouTube							
				Social Posts			Stories			Social Posts			Stories			Non-Skippable			Skippable			Bumper	
Week	Year	Product	Campaign	Gross spends in EUR	Spends n/n/n in EUR	Impressions	Gross spends in EUR	Spends n/n/n in EUR	Impressions	Gross spends in EUR	Spends n/n/n in EUR	Impressions	Gross spends in EUR	Spends n/n/n in EUR	Impressions	Gross spends in EUR	Spends n/n/n in EUR	Impressions	Gross spends in EUR	Spends n/n/n in EUR	Impressions	Gross spends in EUR	Spends n/n/n in EUR
Data source & if required DEFINITION (please specify)																							
W1	2017																						
W2	2017																						
W3	2017																						
W4	2017																						
W5	2017																						
W6	2017																						
W7	2017																						
W8	2017																						
W9	2017																						
W10	2017																						
W11	2017																						
W12	2017																						
W13	2017																						
W14	2017																						
W15	2017																						
W16	2017																						
W17	2017																						
W18	2017																						
W19	2017																						
W20	2017																						
W21	2017																						
W22	2017																						
W23	2017																						
W24	2017																						
W25	2017																						
W26	2017																						

Fig. 10.3 Table format for media landing data across channels and KPIs (own illustration)

Year	ISO Week	Channel	Description *(optional)*	Brand	Product/Line	Gross Spend	GRPs *(optional)*
2020	2	TV	TV Channel "YNews"	Brand ABC	Product 1A	40.000€	50
2020	3	TV	TV Channel "YNews"	Brand ABC	Product 1A	90.000€	150
2020	4	TV	TV Channel "YNews"	Competitor XYZ	Product X5	100.000€	200
2020	3	OoH	-	Brand ABC	Product 1A	100.000€	-
2020	4	OoH	-	Brand ABC	Product 1A	120.000€	-
2020	4	OoH	-	Competitor XYZ	Product X5a	100.000€	-
2020	11	Magazines	-	Brand ABC	Product 2B	60.000€	-
2020	12	Magazines	-	Competitor XYZ	Product X5	55.000€	-

Fig. 10.4 Media landing data per channel split per week (own illustration)

Row	Channel	Description	Currency	TOTAL	National	N1	N2	N3a	N3b	N4	Ost
3					in %						
5	**TV**										
6	Private customer		GRPs	4,650	100						
7	Business customer		GRPs	4,650	100						
8	xxx		GRPs	4,650	100						
9	xxx		GRPs	4,650	100						
11	Private customer		EUR net	3,000	100						
12	Business customer		EUR net	0	100						
13	xxx		EUR net	0	100						
14	xxx		EUR net	3,000	100						
17	Private customers										
19	**OoH**										
20	Permanent	Advertising space Hanover	EUR net	50,000		100					
21	Consumer magazine	Magazine 1	EUR net	16,054		100					
22		Magazine 3	EUR net	16,054	100						
24	**Radio**										
25	FM	classical in Nielsen 2 (20")	EUR net	40,000			100				
27	**Cinema**										
28	Cinemaxx	10x in N1, 15x in N2, 5x in Berlin	EUR net	520,000		33	50				17
29	Cineplex	12x in N1, 18x in N2, 4x in Berlin	EUR net	780,000		35	53				22
32	Business customers										

Row	Channel	January				February				March					
3		1	2	3	4	5	6	7	8	9	10	11	12	13	14
5	**TV**														
6	Private customer	0	0	0	0	150	0	150	150	0	150	150	0	0	150
7	Business customer	0	0	0	0	150	0	150	150	0	150	150	0	0	
8	xxx	0	0	0	0	150	0	150	150	0	150	150	0	0	
9	xxx	0	0	0	0	150	0	150	150	0	150	150	0	0	
11	Private customer	- €	- €	- €	- €	100 €	- €	100 €	100 €	100 €	- €	100 €	100 €	- €	100
12	Business customer	- €	- €	- €	- €	- €	- €	- €	- €	- €	- €	- €	- €	- €	-
13	xxx	- €	- €	- €	- €	- €	- €	- €	- €	- €	- €	- €	- €	- €	-
14	xxx	- €	- €	- €	- €	100 €	- €	100 €	100 €	100 €	- €	100 €	100 €	- €	100
17	Private customers														
19	**OoH**														
20	Permanent	50 €	50 €	50 €	50 €	50 €	50 €	50 €	50 €	50 €	50 €	50 €	50 €	50 €	50
21	Consumer magazine	- €	- €	- €	- €	- €	- €	- €	- €	- €	- €	- €	- €	- €	2,000
22		- €	- €	- €	- €	- €	- €	- €	- €	- €	- €	- €	- €	- €	2,000
24	**Radio**														
25	FM	- €	- €	- €	- €	- €	- €	- €	- €	- €	- €	- €	- €	- €	-
27	**Cinema**														
28	Cinemaxx	10,000 €	10,000 €	10,000 €	10,000 €	10,000 €	10,000 €	10,000 €	10,000 €	10,000 €	10,000 €	10,000 €	10,000 €	10,000 €	10,000
29	Cineplex	15,000 €	15,000 €	15,000 €	15,000 €	15,000 €	15,000 €	15,000 €	15,000 €	15,000 €	15,000 €	15,000 €	15,000 €	15,000 €	15,000
32	Business customers														

Fig. 10.5 Typical media plan as overview table for clients (own illustration)

However, when scaling a modelling approach across countries, product groups, and brands, it is only a matter of time before one faces the challenge of how to deal with "data-poor" allocation units.

An important factor here is the motivation for doing the underlying optimisation. If, for example, the main focus lies on budget optimisation, it may be justifiable—in addition to growth rate and profitability (see Chap. 2)—to simplify the underlying advertising impact curves or, under certain circumstances, to use proxy values:

- Simplifications could include abolishing extensive channel splits in markets having a more challenging data situation. One option might be a rough split into the main groups of media channels as an approximation and more cost-effective solution.
- In countries with a similar customer and media dynamic, the advertising impact curves of reference countries can also be considered as a proxy to provide a pragmatic initial quantity structure of allocation unit (e.g. Sweden as the lead country for other countries in the Scandinavian market cluster)
- In cases where this is not possible, there are approximation methods via expert estimates and benchmark values, for example, from scientific studies. These can then be replaced over time by better estimators (= more comprehensive models).

Broad coverage concerning the allocation units is possible—in a timely manner—through a combination of the described solutions. This could significantly improve the available bases for the planning process in an international marketing organisation.

10.4 Recommendations for Corporate Decision Makers

The proactive management of data and the corresponding templates are levers that decision makers often neglect. It ensures the cost-effective and rapid updating of models and the continuous improvement of the planning basis. In the following, we summarise the most critical success factors.

Organisational success factors

„Data caretaker" from the client-side:
Both from a cost point of view and concerning the medium-term improvement of the underlying reporting processes of relevant data, the early active participation of an employee of the client is an essential factor for the data collection and quality.

Active management of data partners:
The pro-active definition of data templates by clients - instead of relying on, for example, media agencies - provides the basis for efficient reporting of the relevant KPIs. It also enables the client to more easily ensure the consistent provision of the necessary data, e.g. in the event of a change of agency.

Methodological / technical success factors

Continuous improvement of models through strategic data management:
In addition to the current provision of available data, clients should discuss with their service provider the possibilities for improving the data in the future and initiate necessary steps at an early stage. The inclusion of, e.g. additionally available variables then enables a continuous improvement of the forecast accuracy of the underlying models.

Machine-readable data formats and taxonomy:
The customer's data partners should be encouraged at an early stage to provide the necessary information in appropriate data formats to allow the customer cost-effective and straightforward use - not only in the context of MMM projects. Furthermore, a glossary of the relevant variables in the respective files is necessary for promoting consistency and avoiding time-consuming queries.

11 In- Versus Outsourcing and Vendor Selection

The previous chapters have dealt intensively with the methodological aspects of optimising budget allocation in marketing. Once a company has decided to invest in the introduction of advanced solutions in this area, several fundamental questions arise:

- What is the best set-up for a company?
- To what extent should the company build up the necessary skills and capacities in-house?
- Which service provider can support this? In which areas can a company profit from existing solutions (make vs. buy)?

In this context, the implementation success is often strongly influenced by how clear the client is about his use cases and existing capabilities in the early stages. Based on this, a goal-oriented briefing of potential service providers is possible.

This chapter first tries to explain the principle aspects that need to be considered. Based on this, the criteria are presented, which are relevant in a potential provider briefing. Finally, we look at which the dimensions are that should be taken into account when selecting a service provider.

11.1 In- Versus Outsourcing

Depending on the strategic objective and the existing analytical and technical set-up of the company in question, different approaches are possible. Naturally, companies develop over time. What is decisive for the following presentation is exclusively the current situation for the respective company.

In principle, one can distinguish between the following three strategic goals:

S. Stürze et al., *Agile Marketing Performance Management*, Management for Professionals, https://doi.org/10.1007/978-3-658-38053-3_11

- **In-House:** Budget allocation in marketing is a strategic focus topic, and competitive advantage is seen in the strong integration of a corresponding solution into the internal processes and existing tools.
  - Ideally, one has a fully integrated solution into the existing IT landscape.
  - Not only do you have a deep understanding of the underlying models, but you have your own data science resources that allow you to scale and evolve the models.
  - The models are regularly updated via interfaces from which the relevant data is drawn. Ideally, this data is available in a central data lake across countries and brands.
  - The company is considering the support of a service provider as an "accelerator" to set up the solution and a functioning model landscape quickly. But in the mid-term, the company wants to own both the solution and the modelling know-how to operate it.
  - Dynamic budget allocation is an essential part of the digital transformation agenda.
- **Self-service:** Budget allocation in marketing is a strategic focus topic, but there are clear advantages in using a proven solution independently, which a third party is further developing.
  - Ownership of the solution is not the priority, as the aim is to benefit from the know-how of other companies.
  - It is relevant that the necessary development work is done by a third party, which saves the need to build up one's own development resources in this area.
  - The aim is to have a capable team that can best use the results provided and understand and evaluate the underlying models.
  - Ideally, such a solution is web-based and does not require complex integration into one's own IT landscape.
  - A (semi-)automated provision of data is desirable.
  - The company aims to establish a dynamic budget allocation as part of its digital transformation agenda.
- **Advice:** The company wants to benefit from high-quality recommendations in this area without building up relevant resources themselves. Often, a very lean marketing team is looking for a service provider who—due to existing infrastructure—can react quickly to ad-hoc requests as well as to defined scenarios. The requirement is to establish a consistent and integrated marketing ROI measurement across allocation units (countries, product groups, brands) but to have a strong consultant at their side.
  - Model development and updating are on the service provider side.
  - Results and recommendations for action are regularly provided in a classical form via, e.g. presentations.
  - A combination of analysis and consulting services is purchased.
  - The company uses this solution more or less selectively for validation within the planning process.

Figure 11.1 summarises these three strategic orientations:

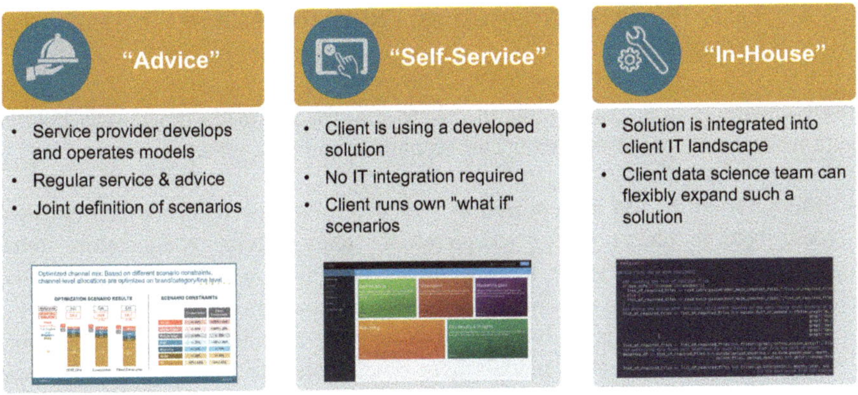

Fig. 11.1 Requirements for service providers depending on strategic goals (own illustration)

- Finally, there is a fourth group: these companies see marketing mix models (MMMs) as helpful, but dynamic planning is not in the strategic focus. The company often uses simple/non-integrated models from partners (e.g. agencies) to look at individual issues. Some companies have simple MMMs across countries and brands, e.g., from one of the established retail panel providers, but do not use them at all or utilise them only sporadically in the context of budget allocation. The company's insight, e.g., into the structure of the models and the data sources used, is often limited.

When changing partners, there is usually no or only a limited transfer of the underlying models and the data behind them. There is only a need for these companies to deal with the evaluation criteria for service providers outlined below when a change to one of the above-mentioned three target stages is considered.

Depending on which strategic goal is the respective company focus, key performance areas and critical capabilities of the service providers are weighted differently. In addition, clarity about the target picture during the tendering process helps to guide the service providers more effectively.

However, if a company is still undecided or uncertain, an RfI (Request for Information) is often placed rather than an RfP (Request for Proposal). This RfI includes broader questions on which the service providers comment.

Part of the process is not only that the service providers present competing solutions. The preferred service provider is often qualified by its ability to best support the client—due to its experience and flexibility—in developing the final strategic approach.

11.2 Early Phase of Orientation: Pilot Studies and First Provider Screening

If a company is in an early phase of orientation, the following points may help to gain more clarity about its own needs, strength, and limitations:

- **The pilot study and data situation:** The core of all solutions are the models—described in the previous chapters—for the individual allocation units. Establishing a pilot study for one of the critical core markets to clarify the availability of the data is crucial to the success and often a "no regrets move". The findings from this study can be used to close potential data gaps and define areas for improvement of models over time. Moreover, such a move does not necessarily commit to a future service provider. After all, based on the data complexity and possible model architecture findings, a client can often submit a more specific request for proposal for its portfolio of markets/product groups/brands to assess different providers in a more meaningful way.
- **The rapid development of the basics versus scaling:** In terms of advanced models and a tool platform for the easy use of the results, it is helpful to use service providers as catalysts. If time is not an issue, cooperations with universities and in-house projects are, of course, an alternative. However, these approaches are understandably often associated with a classic learning curve. Moreover, the availability and fluctuation of employees and know-how transfer can be an additional challenge. Another advantage in using experienced providers is their knowledge across categories and countries. After establishing a successful approach, further scaling with one's own staff remains a valid option.
- **Ownership versus use:** At the start of many evaluation phases, the desire for holistic in-house solution development is a strategic goal. For companies with a high scaling potential and extensive resources in the field of data science, this is also the path to pursue. For many other companies, however, the question arises as to whether a strategy of self-service or advice (see above) concerning the use of critical resources—especially in the area of data science—is not the better alternative in the first few years. Often, the relevant experts in the company are already overworked today, and a corresponding fluctuation in this area represents an additional challenge. With regard to the active and regular use of the results, a self-service option, in particular, offers a good alternative with a minimal burden on the company's experts and a high level of flexibility.
- **Marketing versus IT as project owner:** The advice and self-service options are classic marketing projects. In the case of self-service, only a web-based platform is normally used, e.g., to carry out what-if simulations and analyse the results. This set-up does not require any data science know-how from marketing staff. For in-house projects, it can help to follow a phased approach. In the first phase, the focus lies on creating the content of the models (marketing and data science). In the second phase, this is transferred to a solution in order to access the models via a front-end (solution development, data interfaces, and IS integration). The third

phase often involves international scaling, in which new models are integrated into the existing solution.

- **Initial vendor screening via RfI and pilot markets:** If the client is still unsure which way of doing things is the best, a somewhat broader approach is advisable before developing a comprehensive solution with the final service provider. One option here is to have several potential partners working on pilot markets simultaneously. These are often identified using a two-part questionnaire. On the one hand, questions concerning the detailed aspects of the modelling itself (Sect. 11.3) should principally be considered when selecting a provider. On the other hand, some guiding questions are included to get an impression of the principal approach and of the provider's flexibility. Relevant dimensions for such questions are:
  - **Customer-Front-End (Self-Service)**

    Please describe your front-end solution and how it works (e.g. usage rights, views by user group, real-time simulations) for the different user groups (e.g. global, regional, market, brand teams). What are the main advantages of your solution?

    What requirements does the customer have to fulfil in order to work with this solution? Is installation or training needed?

    Is the respective solution a customer-specific development? If so, to what extent does this solution rely on an existing solution platform?

    Alternatively, is it possible to use an existing standard solution in a licence model? If so, what are the technical requirements? Does the customer benefit from continuous improvements?
  - **Project approach**

    Please describe your approach to a large-scale project (e.g. international scaling), including the division of roles and responsibilities between you and us. Does this distribution of roles differ between pilot and roll-out phases? To what extent do you expect to work on-site or remotely?

    How do you achieve the best balance in terms of consistency between countries, taking into account the relevant differences between them?
  - **Industry experience and client references**

    What experience do you have in optimising marketing budgets between allocation units in general and specifically in our industry? Which relevant clients for comparable projects can you name as references for whom you have recently worked? (Pay particular attention to experience in similar distribution structures, e.g. B2C versus B2B2C, etc.).
  - **Internationalisation**

    Please describe how you approach an international project. Enclosed you will find our top regions/countries and the product groups and brands relevant there.

    How do you deal with "data-poor" countries (see Sect. 10.3)?
  - **Commercial proposal**

    Please give a first indication regarding costs for a pilot project and explain the cost drivers in the context of a possible roll-out.

What are the potential operating costs for the regular use of your services?
What is your cost model for using a front-end solution (SaaS or/and in-house)?
What are the main cost drivers (e.g. amount of media spends, number of users)?
To what extent do you have experience with performance-based fees in the context of these studies? Depending on this, what criteria would you use?

11.3 Technical Evaluation of Service Providers

Regardless of a company's desire to use a front-end solution from a service provider, the underlying models must meet the necessary basic requirements. Key points to be considered in the context of an RfP:

- The provider should offer a dynamic optimisation that allows relevant marketing ROIs to be realised at different levels of the hierarchy (e.g. region, market, brand). Thereby it is crucial to take into account other commercial drivers (e.g. differences in profitability and category dynamics) in addition to marketing effectiveness—see Chap. 2.
- To achieve this, the underlying models should
  - include a list of all relevant variables to ensure a high explanatory content (see Chap. 10),
  - have a high prediction accuracy (MAPE—mean absolute percentage error) for the corresponding target variable, instead of primarily aiming at the statistical quality (see Chap. 6),
  - combine short-term sales and long-term brand effects in an integrated optimisation model to optimise the total impact of marketing investments (see Chap. 3).
- A user-friendly solution is critical to enable regular use and sustainable impact. This solution should allow the quick creation of "what-if" scenarios and a wider group of users to access the results and underlying data.
- A provider should have
  - a consistent model architecture,
  - take a structured approach to ensure acceptance in the organisation quickly; this is particularly important for a possible internationalisation of the solution,
  - be flexible in the solution set-up with the client over time and, e.g., support possible in-housing in the medium term.

The following guiding questions should be adapted by the client as needed to allow service providers to customise their approach to the client's relevant challenges:

- **Use Cases:** Please describe which approaches and underlying analyses you would use to address the following use cases:
  - What is the **right level of spending** to achieve a specific growth target (e.g. volume, net sales, gross profit, number of new customers) at different levels (e.g. global, region, market, brand)?
  - How does your approach help us to better understand the impact of **different spending scenarios** on achieving business objectives?
  - How do you assess the **impact of marketing investments** on short-term sales versus long-term brand effects?
  - How much marketing spend should be allocated to **conventional brick-and-mortar retail compared to e-commerce**? How does one influence the other?
  - How much do the **different sales drivers** (e.g. media, sponsorship, pricing and advertising, customer satisfaction) contribute **to the business and brand objectives**?
  - What is the **optimal mix of media channels**? How much money should be spent on which channel, and what is the **additional benefit of spending €10k more/less on one media channel**?
  - To what extent is it possible to look at the **success of campaigns** in your models? Is this also possible for **online campaigns**?
  - How are the **timings of campaigns** shown by the optimisation? Do we get an optimal distribution of spending over time?
  - How are **halo effects** between lines and categories reflected in your models and model results?
  - Is it possible to optimise between different **target groups** or customer segments?
- **Methodology:** Please describe the methodology behind your approach and also explain how you distinguish between short- and longer-term effects. Feel free to differentiate between the use cases, if necessary.
- **Market clusters and levels:** How would you differentiate between markets differing in data quality? For example, what approach do you take to reflect markets with a lot of data and countries with limited data? When scaling the approach, do you differentiate between core markets and peripheral markets? If so, how?
- **Data requirements:** Please share a list of your data requirements, including necessary granularity (e.g. daily, weekly), necessary history (e.g. last 52 weeks), and from whom you expect this data to be provided (us, you, third parties)? Do you send us data templates?
- **Data automation:** Please describe if and how you approach a cost-effective and low error automation of data submission in case of regular use. If relevant, please distinguish between different use cases (e.g. data-rich vs. data-poor countries).
- **Data landscape and quality:** How do you ensure data completeness and quality? How do you deal with a fragmented data landscape between markets?
- **Cost drivers**
  - What are the relevant cost drivers in the pilot phase? How do you expect these to develop during a roll-out phase?

- What economies of scale can we expect (3 versus 10 versus 50 models)?
- To what extent do you work on a fixed-price basis?
- To what extent do you have experience with performance-based fees in the context of these studies? What criteria would you use?

11.4 Typical Cost Drivers from the Service Provider Perspective

When evaluating the offers—but also before, when describing the requirements and the information and resources provided—it helps to be aware of the cost drivers at issue on the supplier side. The relevant aspects for three typical project phases are looked at in the following:

- **Set-up**
  - A significant cost driver is data collection, integration, and complexity. Up to 70% of the final costs can be attributed to this. The variations between often highly standardised consumer goods manufacturers and, e.g., companies in the financial services sector are sometimes immense. In addition to the possible diversity of data sources and formats, structured data collection in advance by the customer can significantly reduce costs. Furthermore, longer idle times and thus under-utilisation of teams are often a cost factor in the calculations of service providers when they are expect inefficient processes. In most cases, it is more cost-effective to guide standard service providers (e.g. media agencies) or internal departments to more consistent data formats than to pay the modelling service provider for time-consuming data transformations (see Chap. 10 on data formats).
  - High economies of scale often exist within a category (e.g. ten models for 2–3 times the price of a single model). Therefore, it is beneficial for both parties to conduct an extensive pilot of several brands in one category in one market. Usually, it is more expensive to conduct a pilot of a single brand in many markets.
  - Costs for extensive data preparation related to, e.g., the number of models due to product splits or different target variables, should be agreed upon as being optional additional costs, as these details are only needed if the underlying results are satisfactory. A good service provider can often give feedback after the first data assessment to avoid unnecessary additional costs.
- **Scaling across markets**
  - If the underlying sales drivers (see Chap. 6), data sources, and structures are similar, relevant economies of scale can be assumed. Especially in the consumer goods sector, high consistency of data sources can be expected. In this case, it is not unusual that the next five markets can be provided for the cost of one or two pilot markets.
  - If there are significant differences in data depth, activity level, and data providers, it can be beneficial to think about the clustering of markets and

differentiate the analytical approach between them. Comprehensive models are undoubtedly essential for core markets. Experienced service providers often have alternative methods for data-poor markets to include them cost-effectively in an overall optimisation (see Sect. 10.3).

- **Regular operations, data updates, and model refresh:**
  - The main cost drivers here are:
    - the frequency of the updates,
    - whether and how often the models are recalibrated, e.g., to take new media channels into account (see Chap. 6),
    - in which form results are provided (self-service tool versus (semi) standardised PowerPoint slides),
    - the number of simulations and optimisations that the service provider must produce per month/quarter on behalf of the client.
  - Especially for companies with a desired high frequency of data updates (e.g. due to high environmental dynamics), the following constitutes a good idea:
    - a one-time set-up of upload routines and subsequent cost-efficient data update process (e.g. monthly),
    - an easy-to-use front-end that allows the customer to make standard queries based on the latest data on their own,
    - the scaling of such a solution across markets/business units.
  - Thereby, the company should expect from the service provider to distinguish between one-off set-up fees (e.g. depending on the complexity of the data as well as the degree of special requests from the client in terms of reporting and functionalities) and actual maintenance costs (e.g. fixed prices for x updates and y recalibrations within 1 year).

In addition to the cost drivers mentioned above, a factor often underestimated across all project phases is the availability of related project resources on the client side. Providing an internal person responsible for obtaining the necessary data and quickly answering questions regarding content and inconsistencies allows service providers to be significantly more progressive in their pricing. Furthermore, it ensures that the required basic know-how is with the company from the beginning—regardless of whether insourcing is planned at a later point in time.

An experienced service provider should transparently present the elements described in this chapter at an early stage and actively point them out.

11.5 Scorecards for Vendor Pitches

If, based on a tender, a pitch is made by various providers, a basis for objective decision-making is essential. Two examples with different evaluation focuses are presented below.

Table 11.1 first shows an example of a typical list of dimensions that a tendering company collects to record an evaluation of the presented offers. Often the score

Table 11.1 Example of evaluation dimensions of providers (own illustration)

Please rate the provider's presentation and statements in the Q & A session. Below you will find some criteria. Please use a rating scale from 1 to 5: 1 = very good; 5 = very poor.

	Observation level	**Evaluation** 1=very good 5=very bad	**Comments**
1	Understanding of the challenges in the relevant industry and related customer groups		
2	Understanding the category-specific challenges in marketing communication		
3	Scope of the econometric modelling approach and the results behind the tool (e.g., integration of short- and long-term brand effects, forecast quality, optimisation across different allocation units, mapping of different sales channels).		
4	How clearly can the tool guide marketing communication planning (media mix, branding vs tactics, promotion/incentives, etc.)?		
5	Scope and user-friendliness of the presented ROI tool (simulation and optimisation, media planning, data updating)		
6	How suitable is the tool for mapping elements such as international scalability (data-rich versus data-poor markets)?		
7	Plausibility of project plan and schedule		
8	Is there a medium-term possibility of running the tool Independently (vs permanent dependence on the provider)?		
9	Has the provider shown how it can support improving the underlying data and model quality?		
10	Impression of the provider's consulting experience in multinational corporations and complex environments (e.g., centralised & decentralised budgets)		
11	**Overall impression**		

itself is not the prime focus but rather the collection of essential observations and principal assessments by the relevant employees.

The following evaluation matrix (cf. Fig. 11.2), on the other hand, is an example for companies that already have a relatively clear picture of the final scope and the necessary competence profile of their providers. The weightings used need to reflect this preference profile accordingly:

	Customer-relevant dimensions Each item is rated on a scale from 1 (very bad) to 5 (very good)	**Guidelines**	**Number**	**Weighting**	**Provider 1**	**Provider 2**	**Provider 3**
Technical competence (Modelling, AI and front-end architecture)	**Marketing mix modelling competence**	• Several modelling methods in the "toolbox" (not one fits all) • Method selection based on business requirements & data availability • Explicit KPI for measuring model quality (e.g., accuracy, not only R-squared)	1	20			
	Dynamic, self-learning optimisation	• Ability for dynamic, i.e., rolling optimisation and regular automatic recalibration with new data. • Optimisation not only across media channels but also product groups and, if necessary, countries, e.g., taking into account different growth rates.	2	20			
	No black box	• Top management must be able to understand the drivers of the model at all times (i.e., what influence does which driver have) • Transparent treatment of long-term brand effects • The client team can add their own models if desired	3	25			
	Operational know-how	• Demonstrated media know-how • Demonstrated know-how in the operation of the solution • Demonstrated know-how in "hierarchy structures" and budget processes	4	10			
	Support infrastructure	• Maintenance concept (recalibration of models, automatic monitoring of forecasting accuracy, alerting...) • Support concept (customer care, training)	5	10			
	Hosting	• External hosting of the system possible • Deploy on-premise possible on customer systems	6	15			

Fig. 11.2 Example of a typical scorecard for evaluating providers

	Customer-relevant dimensions Each item is rated on a scale from 1 (very bad) to 5 (very good)	Guidelines	Number	Weighting	Provider 1	Provider 2	Provider 3
Implementation competence (User-friendliness, advice, price)	**Reference customers**	• inside and outside the industry • with clear impact evidence • references contactable	7	20			
	Competitive price-performance ratio	• Transparent pricing model, no hidden costs • Separation into set-up and recurring fees (maintenance) • Expected payback in <3 years	8	20			
	Minimised internal effort	• Resources needed in marketing • Resources needed in IT/BI • Realistic data wish list	9	5			
	Iterative time scheduling	• Rapid PoC, e.g., with 1 product group for impact evidence • Afterwards / parallel set-up of the tool • Realistic assessment of the effort for internal data procurement	10	5			
	User-friendliness for marketing (not for analysts!)	• Real self-service tool for marketing • Possibility of simulation at any time ("what-if" scenarios) • Comprehensible representation of the relevant drivers of the model • Optimisation allows the inclusion of manual constraints/guidelines • Display of descriptive analyses, e.g., historical spends	11	25			
	Convincing advisory concept	• Clear advisory approach for setting up the solution • Avoidance of the black box phenomenon (= taking the decision-makers along) • Consultancy approach demonstrates functional and industry understanding	12	25			

Weighting factors	Weight in %	Provider 1	Provider 2	Provider 3
1	20			
2	20			
3	25			
4	10			
5	10			
6	15			
	100			
7	20			
8	20			
9	5			
10	5			
11	25			
12	25			
	100			

Fig. 11.2 (continued)

11.6 Recommendations for Corporate Decision Makers

Once a company has decided to introduce advanced solutions to support agile marketing, a number of fundamental questions arise, particularly regarding the rapid and successful set-up of a solution and finding out which service provider can best and cost-effectively support the project.

Organisational success factors

Clarity about strategic objectives and starting position:
Depending on the strategic objective and the existing analytical setup of the companies, different approaches are possible. In this respect, companies evolve over time. With this, the implementation success is often strongly influenced by how clear the client is about his use cases and existing capabilities. Only then is often a goal-oriented briefing to potential service providers possible.

The rapid development of the basics versus scaling:
Even if the goal is to develop an in-house solution, it can be that with the help of a service provider, this goal can be reached in a faster and more efficient way. It is essential here that the selected partner has the necessary skills to build such a solution as well as the willingness to share the associated know-how with the relevant client staff. In addition, there should be a common understanding of the technical and commercial preconditions under which a developed solution can be handed over and operated by the client.

The path to the goal - via RfI (request for information) to RfP:
Suppose the client is still unsure which approach is most suitable. In that case, a broader approach is advisable before developing the future solution in detail in the main project with the final service provider. One option is to have several potential partners work on pilot cases simultaneously.

Methodological / technical success factors

Use cases:
Based on specific use cases, providers should present which methodological approaches they use to address them.

Data availability and hierarchy levels:
An experienced service provider should be able to adapt the solution approach between data-rich and data-poor countries (heterogeneous data structures). In the context of budget optimisation, the relevant approach should also optimise across different allocation levels (e.g. countries, product groups in a country, multiple brands in a product group in a country, channels within a brand in a country) identify the full optimisation potential.

Marketing in 2023ff: Agility as the "New Normal" 12

Agility in marketing performance management has been a central lever for increasing marketing ROI for years. But especially in times when the business environment is subject to frequent change and decisions have to be made under great uncertainty, it becomes a critical success factor:

- Ever **shorter product life cycles** and a faster succession of product innovations have brought an acceleration to every aspect of marketing since the 1980s.
- **Consumers are changing their behaviour due to changing values** (e.g. vegan food, organic farming, fair trade, work–life balance), new technologies (e.g. iPhone, streaming, video conferencing, e-shopping) or external circumstances (e.g. increased home office use). Calling Customer segments Millennials and Generation Z, for instance, are some of the labels we attach to these changes, changes which are more fragmented and diverse in individualised societies.
- **Digital marketing** was and is a disrupter on both dimensions: Digital marketing channels allow and provoke a greater pace when it comes to resource allocation. In addition, the variety of available digital channels and rapid changes in popularity increases the uncertainty of decisions in marketing performance management.
- Ultimately, the **Corona pandemic**—as is true for many other factors—acted as a catalyst for the above developments.[1]

Driving on sight and frequent recalibration of decisions may have become constant travelling companions. The common denominator of these developments

[1]Did Covid infect Media ROIs? https://analyx.com/did-covid-infect-mediarois/ (retrieved 06/02/2022).

S. Stürze et al., *Agile Marketing Performance Management*, Management for Professionals, https://doi.org/10.1007/978-3-658-38053-3_12

is **an increased need for agile marketing and agile budgeting rather than a decrease in the future. The wheel cannot be turned back.**

Fortunately, driving on sight does not have to be done blindly: Well-structured data are the engine and proven statistical methods based on it are the navigation system for the modern CMO. Three things are key success factors in this "new normal":

1. **Agile budgeting across all levels:** It sounds like a cliché, but without a corporate management driven by an "investor's mindset", marketing will remain a cost centre and talk of ROI will remain lip service. It is necessary to apply the proven principles of digital marketing to the entire playing field: Dynamic (= frequent) reallocation of every marketing dollar to its best use. Instead of just media allocation, also dynamic data-driven optimisation across countries, brands, and product lines. And agile budgeting instead of annual planning.
2. **Agile is not short term:** Agile budgeting should never be confused with short-termism. The goal of all efforts is to maximise the company's profit in the medium term through optimal resource allocation. The latter can and should be agile-adjusted, but with the medium-term profit maximisation in mind. For this, the consideration of long-term brand effects must be an essential part of the toolbox. This applies all the more in times of crisis—may they be caused by pandemics or something else: Coca-Cola significantly reduced its marketing investments in 2020, while P&G, for example, did the opposite.[2] Obviously, the two companies had different assumptions about the effectiveness of their investments.
3. **Marketing needs people:** On the one hand, the new marketing toolbox (data, models, tools) of course needs people who can operate it. This is not an IT task, but belongs in the CMO reporting line. Otherwise, a black box will quickly emerge, which may or may not be trusted. On the other hand, people are needed in the marketing organisation who do not just pay lip service to data-driven decision-making but are ready to be held accountable. Finally, traditional marketing skills will see a new importance: Especially in times of decreasing importance of individual targeting, the notion that the brand-building function of a marketing organisation can be replaced by clicking a few buttons in an ad booking mask at Google is (hopefully) also turning into a thing of the past. Core competencies of a marketing department such as understanding target groups, customer segmentation, and brand management are becoming all the more important again.

All of this requires investments, including strategic data management for high-frequency data and data-driven optimisation technologies based on it, team training,

[2] Ritson, M.: P&G and Coke's pandemic performances prove it: You don't cut ad spend in a crisis; https://www.marketingweek.com/mark-ritson-pg-coke-dont-cut-ad-spend/ (retrieved 06/02/2022).

and external consulting. **But in the vast majority of cases, these investments pay off in less than a year.**

This pleases the CFO and finally gives the CMO tools to quantify his/her value proposition on a permanent basis.

In a few years' time, it may appear completely bizarre that big branded companies at one time had a media plan annually, leaving advertising effectiveness research to their media agency in intervals of several years. The new marketing reality is agile (but not short term), data-driven (but not without a framework), and can demonstrate its own value proposition at any time.

We hope that we have been able to pave a bit of the way towards this new marketing reality with the content of this book.

GPSR Compliance
The European Union's (EU) General Product Safety Regulation (GPSR) is a set of rules that requires consumer products to be safe and our obligations to ensure this.

If you have any concerns about our products, you can contact us on

ProductSafety@springernature.com

In case Publisher is established outside the EU, the EU authorized representative is:

Springer Nature Customer Service Center GmbH
Europaplatz 3
69115 Heidelberg, Germany

www.ingramcontent.com/pod-product-compliance
Ingram Content Group UK Ltd.
Pitfield, Milton Keynes, MK11 3LW, UK
UKHW050058161026
15860UKWH00045B/16
9783658380526